THE BUSINESS CONDOMINIUM

Real Estate for Professional Practitioners
A Wiley Series

DAVID CLURMAN, Editor

THE BUSINESS CONDOMINIUM by David Clurman

THE BUSINESS CONDOMINIUM

A NEW FORM OF BUSINESS PROPERTY OWNERSHIP

DAVID CLURMAN

Assistant New York Attorney General
in charge of cooperative and condominium regulation;
Adjunct Professor of Real Estate,
New York University

A WILEY-INTERSCIENCE PUBLICATION

JOHN WILEY & SONS

NEW YORK • LONDON • SYDNEY • TORONTO

Copyright © 1973, by John Wiley & Sons, Inc.

All rights reserved. Published simultaneously in Canada.

No part of this book may be reproduced by any means, nor
transmitted, nor translated into a machine language without the written permission of the publisher.

Library of Congress Cataloging in Publication Data:

Clurman, David, 1927–
    The business condominium.

    (Real estate for professional practitioners: a Wiley series)
    "A Wiley-Interscience publication."
    1. Real estate business—United States.   2.   Joint tenancy—United States.
I.   Title.

HD255.C53   333.3'3   73-10089

ISBN 0-471-16129-2

Printed in the United States of America

10 9 8 7 6 5 4 3 2

To

LOIS, NANCY, and HEIDI

SERIES PREFACE

Since the end of World War II, tremendous changes have taken place in the business and residential real estate fields throughout the world. This has been evidenced not only by architectural changes, exemplified by the modern shopping center, but also in the many innovative financing responses that have enabled development of new structures and complexes, such as multiuse buildings. It can be expected that new directions in real estate development will speed at an ever increasing pace to match the oncoming needs of our time. With this perspective, the Real Estate for Professional Practitioners Series has been developed in response to professional needs.

As real estate professional activities have become divided into specialties, because of intensive demand for expertise at all stages, so has there developed an increasing need for extensive training and continual education for persons directly involved or dealing in business ventures requiring detailed knowledge of realty procedures.

Perhaps no field of business endeavor is more in need of a series of professional books than real estate. Working in the practical world of business and residential construction and space utilization, or at advanced levels of college training covering these areas, one is constantly aware that too little of existing creative thinking has been transcribed into viable books. Many of the books that have been written do not thoroughly enough encompass both the practical and theoretical aspects of complex subjects. Too often the drive for immediate answers has led to the overlooking of fundamental purposes and technical know-how that might lead to much more favorable results for the persons seeking knowledge.

This series will be made up of books thoroughly and expertly expounding existing procedures in the many fields of real estate, but searching as well for innovative solutions to current and future problems. These books are intended to offer a compendium of each author's wide experience and knowledge to aid the seasoned professional.

The series is addressed to professionals in all walks of realty endeavor. These include business investors and developers, urban affair specialists, attorneys, and the many others whose work involves real estate creativity and investment. Just as importantly, the series will present to advanced students in many realty fields the opportunity to review professional thinking that will help to stimulate their own thoughts on modern trends in housing and business construction.

We believe these goals can be achieved by the outstanding group of authors who will create the books in the series.

DAVID CLURMAN

PREFACE

This book is an effort to help revolutionize much of current thinking on commercial real estate use and ownership. It is my belief that the business condominium may be widely used in the future to attain business goals now impeded by traditional forms of real estate leasing and ownership.

American legislators have enabled the formation of condominium residential and commerical regimes in only the past few years. To date the residential field has received much of the action in condominiums. Nevertheless, examples of business use of condominiums do exist throughout the United States in office buildings, warehouses, shopping centers, professional, medical, and science complexes, and other types of business realty. There is a growing belief among many real estate developers that the business condominium form will find much wider use here in the future, as it has in some foreign countries.

Not only does this book set the possible strategies for the use of condominiums in commercial ventures, it also probes the underlying historical patterns of real estate use and ownership that may be changing in the future with the oncoming use of the condominium.

It is my contention that business groupings in the past have tended to remove independent initiative as companies grew. In lieu of corporations and partnerships that have organized and often smothered individual initiative among participants, the co-venture aspects of condominiums permit independent realty ownership, with cooperative efforts limited to sharing in the use of commonly needed space. The condominium form enables individual proprietorships and firms to seek better locations and wider services that could otherwise mean yielding to mergers, incorporations, and traditional means for pooling efforts that remove individual initiative from some of those concerned.

Leasing procedures are becoming so synonymous with landlord profit sharing that new alternatives will be sought, with the condominium form providing a new and much-needed approach to business real estate adventures.

Developers in the next few years may well consider using the business condominium as the means of obtaining *front money* for development and construction from syndicate investors who will purchase separate offices or floors as condominium unit investors. This may become the new syndication of the 1970s and 1980s.

This book covers the underlying reasons why the business condominium is needed throughout many areas of American business. It probes legal, management, and financial problems involved in the financing, formation, and operation of business condominiums based on my wide experience and research in such endeavors.

I have also attempted to propose unique solutions to some important commercial real estate problems through new uses of the business condominium such as the "sale condoback."

This book has been written with a view toward its use by businessmen and firms seeking expansion involving the utilization of real estate for manufacturing, merchandising, and related activities, especially in the new dimension of development of air space. It should be of considerable interest also to real estate developers, architects, attorneys, brokers, builders, planners, banks, insurers, institutional funds, and others involved in the creative process of constructing, selling, and managing commercial realty. In addition, such professionals as doctors and dentists should be especially interested in the coverage given professional buildings, a form of development that has been becoming quite popular recently, but which needs new thinking and direction. Students in economics, banking, urban planning, real estate, architecture, and related fields on the graduate and undergraduate levels should be aided by the compendium of information, practical proposals, and underlying theory contained in the text.

This book is unique because of the paucity of literature specifically on the business condominium. Even in countries such as Brazil, where there has been extensive use of office building condominiums, there has been little written on the subject. For this reason the book may be of interest as well to real estate developers in the dozens of countries throughout the world in which the business condominium form has taken root.

I hope that my enunciation of theory and practical approach contained in this text will help planners, developers, and investors to achieve new and needed solutions in the development of business realty in the exciting new forms that it will take in the near future. In that connection it is my firm belief that the condominium will play a key role.

Much of the thought involved in sections of this book evolve from my work at the Real Estate Institute of New York University. Nothing contained in this text should be construed as a statement of official policy or view of any government agency.

DAVID CLURMAN

New York, New York
June 1973

CONTENTS

CHAPTER III

STRIDES IN BUSINESS OWNERSHIP OF REAL ESTATE

CHAPTER IV

THE SALE-CONDOBACK

CHAPTER V

MANAGEMENT OF BUSINESS CONDOMINIUMS   74

SUBSTANTIVE BYLAW TOPICAL CHECKLIST   83

CHAPTER VII

SPECIALIZED BUSINESS CONDOMINIUM REGIMES

MEDICAL, DENTAL AND SCIENCE BUILDINGS

INDUSTRIAL PARKS AND COMPLEXES

THE BUSINESS CONDOMINIUM

CHAPTER I

INTRODUCTION

A NEW ALTERNATIVE FOR AMERICAN BUSINESS

An American lawyer visiting a member of the Puerto Rican Bar is stunned to learn that a building housing many prominent law firms is a commercial condominium, with space owned by each firm. In some cases, lawyers seeking only desk space and stenographic and telephone services can only obtain them by participating in the condominium venture.

A sales executive visiting Rio de Janeiro seeking business contacts for his American firm finds building after building owned in condominium form by Brazilian commercial interests. If he wishes only to lease space, the executive is likely to find the lessor to be owner of the office rather than the entire building.

More confusing to the uninitiated might be the division of independent ownership of business space for apparently unconnected purposes. Thus standing on a single parcel of land may be a building divided as a condominium for a separate ground level supermarket, courthouse below ground, and 600-car parking garage rising above ground. Or a commercially run luxury hotel may also house a prestige office building, both owned as a condominium. Such examples are more apt to be found in South America, Europe, and Asia than the United States. But already we can find business condominiums being formed in this country. Although the general public may be unaware that a warehouse is shared in condominium ownership, or that ten doctors and dentists have developed a condominium professional building, astute analysts of business trends are watching this new and exciting development for its more widespread potential and application.

THE CONCEPT OF BUSINESS CONDOMINIUM

The aggressive drive to self-sufficiency and cost-cutting within American business may soon be increased dramatically by development of office building, industrial park, and other business condominiums. The successful test of the residential form of condominium on a large scale has demonstrated the alertness of Americans to new forms of ownership stressing independence, especially compared with established modes of leasing and tenancies. We shall explore the logic for businesses of varied types with general or special requirements to consider as well the occupancy of commercial or industrial space under condominium ownership.

Business condominiums can involve a coupling of independent and common ownership in the entire range of commercial enterprise. For simplicity in introducing the concept, we must first realize that the realm of American business would not be amenable, in most cases, to removal of independence from the core aspect of an undertaking, that is to say, the essential control of the basic business, whether it be commercial or industrial. Thus a manufacturing firm would ordinarily want to retain independent control of key real estate indispensable for product line, output, and basic production functioning. The commonly used realty facilities that are afforded by condominium would most often tend to involve general facilities that could be shared with others, such as a commonly owned warehouse, exhibition hall, recreational facility for employees, railroad siding, or similar property tending to be inordinately expensive if underused because of the nature of the business or its timetable. In a professional medical condominium complex, a battery of X-ray and therapy equipment may be placed in a single area made part of the commonly owned facilities. Arrangements for ownership, maintenance, and scheduling of use of technical equipment would be incorporated in condominium or allied documents.

The condominium arrangement, as in residential housing, thus has two aspects: full ownership of primary space and undivided ownership in other space used together with others. A condominium industrial park typically would have separate pockets of manufacturing space, each held by exclusive outright ownership; but some facilities in the park would be owned and shared in common, with a fractional percentage of undivided ownership being assigned each participant. In an industrial park this could involve common use of parking areas, private roads, sidings, loading platforms, heating and air-conditioning equipment, computers, elevators, garbage disposal and pollution-reduction plants, warehouses, or other facilities capable of common usage for cost-cutting, convenience, or other reasons. The coupling of independent possession with such ownership in common is the hallmark of condominium ownership.

A TOOL FOR SOLVING FUNDAMENTAL BUSINESS PROBLEMS

Most comments on the business condominium thus far have emphasized the increased opportunity presented for the smaller business investor to participate in property in a prime location by buying one floor or one office where he could not acquire an entire building and its site. The passive real estate investor as well as the space consumer who lacks the capacity or need for larger arrangements have been the principal targets for planning of this type.

Reexamination of basic concepts in business economics should also be considered when weighing the potentials of this new form of ownership, with an eye to using this concept as a flexible alternative for major business decisions.

Three gnawing problems permeating wide areas of American business may find relief, or even major reduction, because of the business condominium.

First, the competitive potential of smaller or middle-sized companies could be substantially increased by decreasing major realty and operating costs in the use of condominium ownership that permits a location otherwise beyond reach.

Second, cost reduction in acquiring new plant sites and facilities, as well as elimination of landlord participation when company profits increase, may encourage more experimentation and invention, and faster adaptability to new methods and machines. Opportunities for joint use of machinery located in commonly owned areas may reduce obsolescence problems in some industries that might lead to prohibitive costs for single companies.

Third, conveniences and efficiencies now possible only for giant firms could be obtained through concentration of smaller companies in a condominium complex in which such amenities are shared by joint use of areas owned in common.

Despite antitrust legislation, American business has intensified its trend to concentration of major industries in giant corporations. This result was no doubt inescapable if we consider the need for efficiencies when competing against cheaper world markets and the immensity of cost in introducing and competing against major new products and innovations, both at the manufacturing and marketing levels. The business condominium may present a useful tool for encouraging more and effective competition by middle-sized companies now continually outmoded, outmanuevered, outpriced, and outinvented by giant corporations. Government encouragement of cooperation by small- and middle-sized companies may prove the most reliable weapon in antimonopoly policy.

Plans for generating new businesses in depressed areas, encouragement of minority ownership, may be widened by effective use of the business condominium concept, even if government plays a business role. Consider the wide possibilities from a group of small machine part producers in a ghetto area who are enabled to own an interest in a common parking, loading, or warehouse area, rather than to operate, typically, in abandoned stores, choked off from essential production techniques by lack of such facilities. In many situations only a small increase to each firm in the investment capital aid by government or private banks, with a change to business condominium, could alter the business outlook, and even the face of the community, in a way that could achieve business and social results now largely unreached because of the lack of imaginative planning.

One may argue: why can't a landlord provide a wide range of commonly used facilities in addition to traditional services? Yet, as we see particularly when focusing on shopping centers and industrial parks (where landlords regularly do provide some commonly used areas and conveniences), such key concepts as management control, favoring priorities for different occupants, and profit motivations take different directions when orientated for unit owners rather than tenants. We seriously question whether landlords can provide the quality of services and independence, irrespective of the physical plants they build, that a condominium regime allows.

Then there is the problem of landlord economics. A landlord projecting construction of a broad spectrum of commonly used tenant facilities must concern himself with additional management costs, repair and replacement charges, calendars for use, arbitration of disputes among tenants, a larger initial investment and long-term debt cost, and probably much less flexibility in attracting the different occupations underlying his rent roll. He must correctly predict that future tenants will want the extra space set aside for common use. In some instances, his operating costs for the same facilities may be higher than for a condominium. For example, shorter-term tenants might not be expected to care for the commonly used facilities in any manner that would approach those of occupants with a more direct financial and prestige interest in the longevity and ownership of such common facilities. A condominium unit owner, who by definition is also an investor, may be willing to pay for additional commonly used conveniences. Many businesses may not be willing to do so as mere tenants with no substantial controls over management.

Growth in development of business condominiums may force competing developers of rental buildings to provide broader services for tenants, including common area availability. If such eventuality comes about, we may expect many newer buildings to be converted later, conveniently, to a condominium. Democratic control of common areas possible for tenant purchasers, as well as escape from such burdens as percentage rent clauses, would be among the important factors influencing tenant purchases.

HISTORICAL PRECEDENTS

What historical roots have led to thoughts of condominium helicopter platforms and hangars operated and owned by several corporations? When unused mountains become ringed with swirls of condominium freight-carrying monorail systems developed as part of the business community in a new town on the countryside, where do we find historical data and treatises that show us how these condominium came to be?

Businessmen for hundreds of years have sought after wealth and power by devising and structuring forms of ownership and trade conducive to the problems of their times, often involving a combination of efforts. Docks, quays, storage rooms, and record-keeping offices were operated in shared participation by the guilds of the early Middle Ages. More aggressive successors, interested in outbounding mere local trade, stretched out combined efforts for national and international trade and commerce by establishing powerful joint trading, shipping, and exploration companies, joint banking associations to finance group participants in new ventures, even joint transportation companies to control and protect navigable waterways. Colorful names abound: the merchants corporations of France, the liveries of England, the Hanseatic League of Germany. Besides the better known common meeting places and exchanges for such merchants and investors who usually owned and operated a great deal of business property independently, considerable joint use was made of business facilities essential or incidental to efficient business operation by participants.

Walled towns and enclosures of early Europe were as much protection for tradesmen and their centers of marketing as for other residents. In fact, many of these towns were organized or chartered at the behest of tradesmen for their common protection, with erection of fortresslike walls itself a common business venture. Levies on local tradesmen chiefly maintained and guarded the walls in their beginning history. With this background one might say that early charges and taxes on business property owners aimed at general maintenance of commonly used facilities in some of the earliest towns have the ring of condominium participation—independent ownership of space with a sharing of interest and cost in commonly used facilities. Mainly the formalities and nomenclature of undivided common interest ownership are missing.

Just as condominium, or "storied" division of buildings on commonly used land, developed by custom to enable residential ownership of upper stories in walled areas, the tradesmen of the time similarly were often forced to intensify use of commercial facilities. Both the shortage of space in walled areas and the enormous importance of business location at core points or market centers intensified the sharing of prime space.

Early drawings and prints of life in walled towns picture large trading rooms separately enclaved for different merchants, common storage bins holding inventories and supplies of many traders and artisans, and other evidence of commonly used facilities in the tall, timbered structures that shadowed the narrow streets of medieval Europe.

Whereas early condominium residences emphasized the *independent* aspect of ownership of storied property (largely a Franco-Germanic concept), a direct result of land shortage in walled towns, the businessman emphasized *joint* cooperative use of common facilities in trading centers because of the same land shortage. Joining a guild, trade company, or hanse meant sharing by merchant custom and license in commonly used marketing, storage, or transportation centers. From this early kind of essential pooling of efforts came the more formally chartered or organized partnership and joint-venture company. However, a great amount of individuality and enterprise control was sacrificed in most of these efforts at grouping. The cooperation of tradesmen for mere convenience in personal creativity gave way later to commonly run activities that overshadowed any remnants of individual choice of product, pricing, or distribution.

This absorption of the individual has become commonplace. It is ironic that some of the most vocal, rugged-individualism champions in the world have been multinational corporations, trusts, and corporations whose own creation and growth was through constant group absorption of individual creativity and scotching of independent competitive initiative.

It is hoped that those who consider the potential for the business condominium will note the tendency to emphasize individual initiative in its use, without cooperation among businessmen dampening its under-lying motif of independence. The practicality of cooperative business effort need not always lead to smothering of individual company initia-tive, takeovers by larger companies, restraint of trade and monopoly, all concepts that have resulted from existing pooling methods.

The thriving existence and legal sanction given to the corporate form, the partnership, the trust, and other associations are indicative of the enormous need for the combination of efforts and pooling in American and international business. It is not combination per se that is wrong; it is its misuse. A wide variety of old and new business forms and legal organizations is vital to cope with the economic and social demands of modern civilization.

With most forms for business enterprise there is scant opportunity to combine with others without losing substantial individual control and initiative. Joining together in the same business corporation, trust, or partnership is usually tantamount to yielding to majority rule or other controlling interest. Mergers of business firms customarily involve an absorption of individualism in favor of group interest. Even business coop-eratives, originally founded to fight back at big business and fixed rail and other rates, often thrive on controlled production, fixed pricing, and regulated marketing.

If used wisely the business condominium can be the first new entry in the business form parade that emphasizes individuality while benefit-ting from cooperative business efforts. But the cooperation here, by the very nature of the concept, need not mean surrender of product line and method of manufacture, price dictation by others, and regulated marketing methods.

It is ridiculous to conclude that all important forms of business organi-zation have been invented previously and that we are thereby limited. Ours is an age when young people steam from the frustrations and depri-vations of past delays and inequities—sometimes resulting from plodding and wasteful activities of major business incapable of rapid change for fear of loss of revenue or hardened habits.

There are already signs that the real estate business is searching for new forms for doing business. The growth of the real estate investment trust (REIT), a creature given life by the Internal Revenue Code in 1961, evidences the constant need for reevaluating the adequacy of exist-ing business forms. A chief purpose of the REIT, as popularly called, was elimination of traditional double-level corporate taxation for group-ings of real estate investors. In the tight-money real estate market of the late 1960s, over a billion dollars of important construction and devel-opment financing was pumped into the market place by mortgage REITs.

The business condominium also may become a valuable tool for the legitimate conduct of business, even a commonplace form of accepted business organization. Perhaps chief among its benefits, in addition to dollar-and-cents opportunities, will be the furthering of individual business initiative. It is a method that looms promisingly for both social and business opportunities.

UNDERLYING REASONS FOR BUSINESS CONDOMINIUM

Most decision making that involves consideration of use of the business condominium form usually relies on one or more of five underlying reasons for reviewing this new choice of business enterprise.

1. Opportunities for diversification.
2. Need for specific, limited locations.
3. Convenience in operations from supporting facilities.
4. Cost efficiencies.
5. Investment opportunity.

OPPORTUNITIES FOR DIVERSIFICATION

A key problem clouding business thinking on diversification is the need for substantial outlay of funds on a relatively long-term basis supported by capital investment in plant or similar facilities that may involve expensive new construction, large debt undertakings for mortgages, and limited opportunity for inexpensive recall of the undertaking.

Several possibilities loom for condominium. Let us look at a set of circumstances that may prove commonplace before long. A medium-size manufacturing company has decided that more space is essential for its primary production. At the same time, the firm has decided to experiment with diversification by adding a newly invented product to its manufacturing line. A major land purchase is made, and facilities are constructed to house the production of the regular and new products. But the dual facilities are carefully kept separate, so that the new product portion of the plant could be sold off separately at a future date. In such eventuality, a business condominium would be formed for the entire site, to permit the business spinoff while retaining independent control of regular manufacturing facilities, with common sharing of jointly used facilities incidental to both condominium units thereby created. Without planning for a condominium, the company might end up with wasted or underused, expensive space.

In another case a condominium unit owner wishing to test manufacture a new product may decide to expand on a small scale within present confines, thereby taking advantage of existing warehouse, location, and other facilities not otherwise available except at prohibitive expenditures. If the new product proves successful, normal expanding procedures can be followed thereafter, either by buying more condominium space or by separate development elsewhere.

NEED FOR SPECIFIC, LIMITED LOCATIONS

Oftentimes businessmen find there is just nowhere else to go but a specific locale for conducting their businesses. An industry-wide custom may have developed of centering operations, in entirety or in a special aspect such as product exhibition, by locating in a trade center for the particular kind of business. Furniture, furs, textiles, and jewelry trades have notably been so concentrated in several American cities. In other cases there may be vacant space in several locations, but the most desirable is in a prestige area uplifted by sophisticated surroundings in an attractive setting most conducive to the business activity of the company. There are also instances in which the limitation of choice is fixed by local zoning or a traditional business district border.

Purchasing a business condominium for *part* of such vital space can bring a company a needed location with needed independence of ownership and future confidence, without the immense cost of purchasing land and an entire building.

CONVENIENCE IN OPERATIONS FROM SUPPORTING FACILITIES

Proximity to railroads, airports, or harbors may necessitate location for convenience in operations. In some South American cities in which the business condominium has been used for office space, the concentration of office space is substantially conditioned by difficulties in reaching hinterland plants, communication limitations beyond certain city zones, and inclement climate outside of coastal regions.

In new towns which will soon fill previously undeveloped land in the United States, it is quite likely that office and industrial complexes will be planned and built to utilize preconceived conveniences of transportation, communication, and labor supply. The business condominium may be utilized here to encourage permanence of new or relocated businesses, with a host of convenient amenities being offered industry as encouragement for moving to the new location.

COST EFFICIENCIES

Elimination of a landlord may bring down existing and contingent costs. Most rentals have escalation factors in the ordinary variety of lease arrangements. Either rentals automatically escalate by increases in the landlord's burdens, such as realty taxes or mortgage charges, or increases are tied to new services required by the lessee, or increases are fashioned at regular intervals by market determinations of higher landlord rate of return.

In recent years many consumer sales companies have found profits diluted by lease clauses granting landlords profit-sharing rights under percentage leases. In effect, the lessor becomes a partner to future increases in income. Many businesses, even larger ones, find it almost impossible to rent substantial space for retail outlets without incurring percentage rental obligations. The potential dilution of profits can be immense.

The business condominium presents the opportunity to eliminate this increasing burden on firms developing increasing business.

INVESTMENT OPPORTUNITY

The business condominium may provide the vehicle to bring the medium- and small-size real estate investor back into the market place from which he has been barred as an independent operator by skyrocketing land and construction costs.

The purchase of units in such enterprise may well be handled by smaller investors who have been practically removed from participation in real estate investments of certain types, including new construction and prime existing properties in good location.

Constructing a business condominium for many investors who will take floors or rooms for investment holdings presents an alternative to the typical limited partnership syndicate in vogue at the present time. Rather than a passive approach, some investors may wish to obtain valuable space within a large complex that they can promote and manage themselves. It may also be possible to safeguard investments better by more careful scrutiny of management in its handling of a specific condominium unit rather than when a general, undivided investment in a syndicate is made in which the general partner has extremely broad discretion over a large single property.

For the developer, the syndication by condominium unit sales presents the opportunity to obtain additional "front money" for construction and development purposes that he would not be able to capture if a rental or full-ownership project were planned. The amounts received will reduce the developer's risk capital as well as diminish construction loan costs.

Some European examples have begun to bear more directly on the American real estate market. For example, developers in some European countries have been attempting to form business condominium investment groups, some involving over a hundred investors per enterprise, to purchase land to build office buildings in the United States, with offices separately owned by each overseas investor. The offices would be leased to American tenants who would pay the rentals through an appointed managing agent. Besides specific income tax benefits available to investors in certain countries from this construction and ownership technique, such as Germany, the method also has grown out of the shortage of construction loans in many foreign countries that do not have the immense depositories of savings held by American institutional lenders that support the mortgage market for construction and development funds. The use of the syndication technique by Americans within the United States, where formidable mortgage lending may be added to the method, truly presents interesting possibilities.

The business condominium, through sale of separate investment units, may well help create a breakthrough for wider public ownership of real estate in years to come. This may prove to be the new syndication of the 1970s and 1980s, worldwide in its dimensions.

CHAPTER II

STRUCTURING A BUSINESS CONDOMINIUM

AN ENABLING STATUTE

American condominium statutes were in the first instance enacted primarily to create a new format for residential use. For that reason, some doubt may remain even now as to their coverage of entirely commercial enterprises. In the main, by a variety of language, most jurisdictions would appear to permit business condominiums to be submitted to their respective state statutes.

Some condominium laws elaborate permitted business uses in broad terms, covering "the operation of any industry or business." There are laws to such effect in Alaska, Arizona, Arkansas, District of Columbia, Hawaii, Indiana, Iowa, Kentucky, Louisiana, Maryland, Michigan, Nebraska, New Jersey, North Carolina, Oklahoma, South Carolina, South Dakota, Tennessee, Texas, Virginia, and Washington. California and Colorado also cover the broad range of commercial use by somewhat different language.

Some states define a "unit" or "apartment" in a condominium as intended for "any type" of independent use, as do Connecticut, Georgia, Illinois, Kansas, Minnesota, New Mexico, Pennsylvania, Rhode Island, Utah, and Wisconsin. Although the word *apartment* in some statutes may sound like residential use to an American ear, this should not bar commercial ownership where the word is used instead of *unit* (as in Georgia, Kansas, Minnesota, and New Mexico). The word *apartment*, or *apartamento*, had been used for business units in Europe and South America for a considerable time before being copied into American statutes.

New York permits any type of "use or uses" for its condominiums. Florida's broad definition of a unit merely provides that it must be "a part of the property which is subject to private ownership." The laws of Nevada and Mississippi are to the same effect as Florida, with somewhat different language.

In the Massachusetts statute the word *building* is defined to require a "structure designed for dwelling or office purposes, private or public." Although a valid motivation for this approach presumably was encouragement of office condominiums in Boston and other large cities, one wonders whether this language barred, in effect, all business condominiums other than offices. Or, are all locations, for whatever purpose, of any business venture, *offices?*

THE BUSINESS PURPOSES

Assuming that a state statute empowers registration of a business condominium in a particular locality, an early decision should be made as to general or specific purposes intended. This procedure assures that zoning questions are raised promptly, and makes for more explicit salesmanship.

A master document called a declaration or "master deed" must be filed by the originating property owner submitting his premises to the condominium form of ownership. Many essential elements are specified that will, practically speaking, permanently govern the operation and direction of the undertaking in this new form of ownership. One of the more important representations in that document, filed pursuant to law, is the intended use of the land and building now submitted to condominium. Although condominiums that are all residential pose little problem delineating use, the commercial condominium presents more complex questions because of the gamut of undertakings involving commercial enterprises.

The author has read a filing for a condominium of several warehouses that stated the use to be that of "manufacturing" with no additional comment. "Office use" is use terminology sometimes found for buildings where light manufacturing is not intended to be proscribed, without elaboration of the latter fact.

Quite often the particular initial uses are represented in too specific categories, with no provision for unrelated businesses, as for example, "to be used as a restaurant in Unit A and otherwise for the printing business in the other units." What if the restaurant owner fails in business and wishes to sell his unit to a printing company? Sometimes the effect is just the opposite, with almost unlimited use permitted by the filed declaration of intention, as for example, "first and second and third floor condominium units, A, B, and C may be used for any business, commercial, or industrial purpose otherwise not prohibited by law."

In the absence of clarity in original documents or later consent of a requisite number of unit owners to amend the declaration regarding use of premises, there appears to be little statutory aid in the United States to guide solution of dilemmas caused by some forms of limitations or vagueness as exemplified by instances cited above.

In France, a unique provision in the Law of July 10, 1965, (Article 8, Chapter I, Law Number 65-577) governing condominium ownership may be helpful to reach solutions to controversies arising out of this type of problem. That section states: "The declaration (réglement de copropriété) cannot impose any restriction on the rights of unit owners other than justified by the purpose (destination) of the building as defined in its documents, in accordance with its characteristics or its location."

The French law may well provide a reasonable rule for interpreting American problems in this area that must arise in cases where documents are poorly drafted or little concern is evidenced for future problems as the result of shortsightedness.

STATUTORY PURPOSES FOR BUSINESS CONDOMINIUMS

Prior to the existence of enabling legislation, principally enacted since 1960, the business form of condominium was almost nonexistent. Without statutory protection for this form of business organization, substantial complexities and dangers would exist. This is demonstrated by an examination of the protective purposes of condominium statutes as related to business enterprises.

The function of such statutes in this connection would mainly be:

1. To ease the transfer of property interests without the necessity of long, involved descriptions of ownership.

2. To prevent severe business dangers that might ensue from dividing or partitioning property intended for independent or common use.

3. To superimpose on contractual arrangements basic and fair relationships and procedures with respect to business operations.

4. To set standards, conditions, and limitations on condominium real estate that would permit mortgage lenders to make loans secured by such interests.

5. To require separate and equitable real property assessment by government on individual unit owners.

6. To provide the mechanism for the filing of basic registration and conveyancing documents in official places.

In the case of business condominiums, the requirements for elaboration and specification of individual interests may involve the composition of considerably more detailed filing documents than for residential realty. This is because of the likelihood of substantially varying types of business enterprises, each containing characteristics needing special protection. However, the basic definitions and mandated requirements for condominiums in the statutes serve to protect the organization of the business condominium, especially in areas of general importance, such as organizational procedures and compliance with provisions enabling the mortgaging of properties and the issuance of title insurance policies.

FILING THE MASTER DECLARATION

An owner of a parcel of real property who has decided to offer condominium units does, in effect, subdivide his property before offering it. Prior to his conveyance of the first condominium unit to be sold, the entire venture, including all condominium units described in the declaration, are fully owned by the developer. Mere solicitation of interest in a condominium to be formed does not of itself create a condominium. Deeds to condominium units cannot validly be issued until a declaration or "master deed" has been registered with the appropriate government authority, which enables transfer, thereafter, of individual condominium units.

The basic condominium document, the declaration, sets forth the multitude of relationships upon which the condominium rests. The declaration describes in detail the location and specifications of each unit, the relationships among the unit owners, and other essential information concerning the business condominium.

STATUTORY SAFEGUARDS

Two fundamental safeguards appear in most condominium statutes. One bars "partition" of the real estate otherwise available to owners of undivided interests in common. If such procedure were available in condominiums, any business owner could quite freely petition and obtain from a court the physical division of real estate involved, or a court order for the sale of the particular property. In a business condominium, such an act would be intolerable, and its possibility could jeopardize ventures of this type.

Similarly, the condominium statutes forbid the division of the two forms of real estate ownership held by a condominium owner—an independently owned area and an undivided interest in the common elements. The laws require that the package remain intact and forbids the ripping apart of these two aspects of ownership that combine to make for the condominium deed. Thus a unit owner cannot sell off his fractional share in the common interests. To provide otherwise would violate the underlying concept of condominium ownership.

VARIABLES IN BUSINESS VENTURES

There are three factors often subject to variation during the life of business condominiums, which should be thoroughly explored prior to structuring this new form of ownership.

1. Cost changes.
2. Variations in use of originally conveyed space.
3. Additional land or building space needs for expansion.

COST CHANGES

At the origination of the condominium, when the declaration is filed, some formula must be fixed for determining the allocation of common charges to the participants in the condominium venture. In residential realty the most common purchase procedure is to fix a pro rata method based on the relationship of prices charged, that is to say, the original value relationships. In other cases in residential condominiums the amount of floor space is the determining factor in the allocation of responsibility for common charges. Condominium statutes permit separate mortgages to be placed on units as well as separate tax assessment for payment of local taxes. For these reasons, the residue made up of common charges is largely for the purpose of sharing in the maintenance upkeep of the common areas applicable to the condominium. It is common practice to fix charges per unit based on the respective interests owned in the common elements. Original value or floor space are the two most common mathematical standards.

What should a fair determination of cost sharing be? Commercial space on a rental basis is ordinarily set on the basis of a floor-space determinant, often per square foot. It is also common practice to increase the rental by charging more for floor space in prime areas, as on higher floors of a high-rise office building. With this traditional background, a substantial number of business condominiums will have common charges allocated based on floor space per unit. Whether the determination will also be based on the greater or lesser value of location of the floor space might also be considered in making the mathematical breakdown of common-charge responsibility.

One wonders whether such a floor-space concept is adequate in all situations. Should common charges be based on the fairness in covering expenses or on the supposed value relationship of the premises? If the former be the case, then a mere floor-space determination without a location factor may be reasonable in many cases.

Cost factors are much more difficult to predict for business condominiums than for residential kinds. Commercial expense aspects are extremely changeable, especially if the business ventures are of the manufacturing or industrial type. In addition, the difficulty in predicting realistic cost burdens is heightened when the business condominium includes radically different forms of business enterprise, such as a combination of an office building, manufacturing plants, or restaurants. Some units may make exorbitantly more use of common areas than others and have, in effect, exclusive use of other areas that are expensive to maintain. For the aforesaid reasons, it may be necessary to include some factor for redistribution of cost responsibility at a later date based on an audited compilation of actual cost experience. Current statutes may generally block such approach.

There are other substantial statute problems in requirements for derivation of cost formulas. In some states condominium statutes may bar use of floor-space formulas entirely, usually limiting the method to some form of value relation of units to overall property. In other states common interests must be shared equally, one for each unit. Yet in other states there is wide freedom in original allocation of common interests, with no real formula specified. In New York an allocation based on floor space is expressly permitted by statute (subject to reflection of exclusive advantages in parts of common elements enjoyed by some unit owners).

It is an open question whether floor-space allocations must be completely uniform throughout a building or can be subject to a value ratio based on the location or use of exclusive space or common elements.

It is suggested that, wherever possible, statutes be reasonably construed to the latter effect, to accommodate in a logical way some of the foregoing allocation problems in business condominiums.

If commercial ventures are impeded by existing statutory bars that prove unresponsive to reasonable business development, changes should be considered.

VARIATIONS IN USE OF ORIGINALLY CONVEYED SPACE

Business unit owners may very well be concerned with the degree of mutually contracted obligation by one another to continue the same forms of business enterprise. For example, the question of an owner adding a new line of business at a later time that would be in competition with another unit owner is an open possibility in many cases. A condominium high-rise shopping center could begin with a second floor woman's apparel store specializing in maternity clothes. Query whether this unit owner would enjoy a change from a luggage business above him to female maternity clothing.

There may come a time when an individual unit owner finds that his space is just too large and wasteful for his continued operation and wishes to contract either to sell part of this space or to lease it. Will the other owners have the right to purchase outright some of this space? If so, what will be the order of priority if several are in need of such additional area?

If a passive investor purchases a unit to lease for income, what mechanical formula will be used for payment of common charges? Can *net* rent arrangements be made whereby the unit owner's tenant pays all such charges and merely pays an additional agreed rental to the owner, net of enumerated expense burdens?

The question of use also will relate directly to types of equipment permitted on the premises, even if the original business or industry is continued without change by the original purchaser. It is possible that the special design of new equipment may substantially change the nature of a building and affect resale value of other units. Thus noisy printing equipment added to a firm that had operated previously with chemical or photography reproduction methods may substantially disturb others coming in and out of the building.

We can expect additional problems from subsidiaries of large corporations, or firms acquired as such, in which new management policy may change the flavor and flow of business activity on the premises. For that reason also, predictability is much less possible in contemplating the direction of a building than in the residential field.

ADDITIONAL LAND OR BUILDING SPACE NEEDED FOR EXPANSION

The business condominium can be limited as to land and building area, or it can have a surplus of unused property subject to future expansion arrangements, or it can have land that is noncontiguous and expandable. Expansion problems are often cited by opponents of commercial condominiums. There is no doubt that this is an important problem, yet it is doubtful that it is as important as sometimes indicated.

Most firms who enter into condominium arrangements generally do so with respect to foreseeable circumstances. Quite often the availability of resale value puts the participant into a position essentially no different than when he operates in a rented or entirely owned situation and finds that he needs more space. The answer is similar—he moves to where he will have more space.

The rental tenant is often pressured by a particular time schedule to decide to stay or move, the date of lease termination bearing down on decision making. However, he does not have to spend time looking for a purchaser of space, which may prove expensively time consuming, unless he is seeking an assignee of his lease. In the latter situation, the problem of landlord consent can be a delaying and obstructive factor.

The condominium unit owner is not under the same time pressure when considering removal, because of the absence of a lease termination date. Assuming a marked degree of freedom to transfer ownership, the unit owner may often find himself in a more flexible position for withdrawal than if he had held tenant status. The condominium form of ownership also might actually work to additional advantage in some instances, because the unit owner may be enabled to use an appreciation of property ownership value as the basis for financing expanded quarters. In addition, arrangements can possibly be made that could give some leeway where expansion is necessary. The condominium can leave some space unused or used for facilities that could be altered where expansion is necessary. If the condominium is expandable, it is possible that construction can take place that need not be contiguous to the original property. Thus a condominium made up of several light industry plants that find the need for wider employee parking facilities could, by unanimous agreement, purchase parking space within walking distance, even though it is not contiguous.

There is less need for contiguity in the case of business condominiums as distinguished from residential condominiums. And it is quite likely that dispersement will solve some of the expansion problems in years to come. Eventually single-business condominiums may even be spread into different cities, states, and countries.

DIVISION OF CONDOMINIUM UNITS

Zoning and building codes may be expected to clash with attempts to divide condominium units of a residential type into a group of smaller units providing residences for a number of families rather than the original one. However, use restrictions are ordinarily much less stringent in zones where commercial and industrial structures are allowed. It is not uncommon for floor space used in entirety by a prior commercial occupant to be divided to accommodate several business occupants within the same space.

Space subdivision possibilities should be faced when structuring the business condominium, both for future changes and to correct original marketing misjudgments of space divisions that will sell. Probably because of the easy tendency to copy from residential condominium documents when designing commercial space, this one differing aspect of business ventures is often largely overlooked. Consequently, the right to subdivide, if it is to exist, should be authorized by the declaration, perhaps by language such as:

The Unit A unit owner at any time is hereby empowered to divide such unit into two or more units, and may transfer, convey, sell, or assign such new units without further consent or approval of the then Board of Managers or any unit owner or unit owners; provided that such new units are first fully described and delineated in an amendment duly filed to the declaration made by the dividing owner of Unit A, which amendment shall contain new floor plans, specifications, tax lot numbers, and other requirements of the condominium statute, duly certified as per such requirements, as if part of the original declaration; and provided further, that such new units shall be expressly subjected in such amended declaration to all terms and conditions of the declaration and bylaws, including the obligation for payment of common charges. In such situation the total of all new unit percentages of common interests in common elements and obligation for common charges shall be exactly the same as that applicable to the original unit before division.

Division should not result in increasing or decreasing the total common interests and maintenance obligations applicable to the unit originally, as possessed by the divider himself. Good practice would also necessitate description in the original declaration of the rights of dividers and their assignees to remove partitions, redecorate, and so on, consistent with the uses sanctioned by the declaration and bylaws. However, if bylaws mandate board permission in special instances involving possible detriment to others in the condominium venture, it may be well to carry over this requirement to protect the character of the building.

If the declaration is silent on division of units, it is doubtful that any existing condominium statute would empower unilateral subdivision by any unit owner. In most cases, by law or by original governing documentation, the unanimous consent of all unit owners will probably be essential, thus highlighting the urgency of careful analysis when the business condominium is structured.

Divisionability of units must be a key concern to passive investors purchasing original units for leasing purposes or eventual resale. Mortgage lenders also would acquire more valuable security if given the additional right to divide units on foreclosure; moreover, the unit appraisal value is also heightened.

An original developer who reserves the right to divide unsold units is positioned to correct poor market projections made before construction. By formalizing his right to divide in the declaration, he avoids the quandaries of unanimous consent requirements from unit owners who already hold conveyances of business units.

PHYSICAL SEPARATION OF UNITS

Structuring of the business condominium occasionally discloses another element more complicated than that in the residential form, the nonuniformity in physical separation of independently owned areas. In office building condominiums the principles tend to follow lines similar to apartment residences. Inside or outside walls or partitions, and under or outer sides thereof, are typical dividing lines. By such set borders relative independence and certainty are obtainable with clarity in evaluation of the adequacies of condominium ownership. Total office buildings will ordinarily have relatively uniform division of utility and heating feeding systems, thereby easing planning for the division of internal maintenance responsibilities on an equitable basis.

In proposed business condominiums, it is insufficient to plan for independent ownership based merely on comparative floor space occupied if there are wide differentials of height and load capabilities among the units. Measurement of ownership becomes more complex if the various units possess wide differences in space distributions, such as height or specialized protrusions. For example, a lower unit having exclusive right to a loading platform could very well be independently owned from a point beginning with an inside wall that is extended to the end of a loading platform, or even to a cement surface beyond. If the intervening outer walls in such case are made common elements, then the distribution would have to except the outer walls. In many cases, the use of the restricted or limited common element concept, by which exclusive use of a common element is given to a particular owner, is helpful in avoiding the complexities in describing the total area used exclusively as an independent unit.

UNITS AS COMMON ELEMENTS

It is sometimes advisable to set off as an independent unit an area used for joint operations by all or several condominium unit owners. If all owners make similar use of the area, the common charges can be allocated to cover costs of machinery, operations, and maintenance, and establishment of a separate unit may not be necessary. On the other hand, if only a few unit owners make use jointly of such an area, they alone should bear responsibility for its cost. Because state laws often do not permit allocation to unit owners of common charges other than on a unit-value or unit–floor-space basis, it would seem difficult in such cases to assess additional payments as common charges from only some of the unit owners. Therefore, by creating a separate unit owned in partnership by the few utilizing unit owners, such costs can be equitably allocated.

HIGH-RISE VERSUS HORIZONTAL DEVELOPMENTS

When determining the extent of independent ownership of units a foremost thought relates to the allocation of common charges, if the formula for such charges relates to the extent of floor-space ownership. Such a question is less important in horizontal business condominiums with separate heating, electrical, and other utility facilities. This situation permits separate billing for many items that would have to be includible as common charges in a high-rise structure, with the exception of provision for separately metered services. Where a wide difference exists in a high-rise building in the use of commonly owned facilities, such as a central heating and the electrical system, the metering of separate units will not take care of the problem of payment for periodic repairs and replacements that fall as a common obligation. The problem of assessment for replacement cost must also be considered with reference to the primary users of such equipment.

RETENTION OF SPACE BY BUILDERS OR DEVELOPERS

In a considerable number of business condominiums developers have retained sizeable portions or area within or contiguous to the business condominium for their own use, either for rental purposes of units or for direct operational activities. For example, the restaurant area of an office building condominium could be retained by the developer as a separate condominium unit for rental purposes, to achieve additional income. Just as possible, the builder may carve out of the land involved a separately owned parcel that is not part of the condominium, either for his own operations or for rental purposes.

MOBILE UNITS

The increasing use of mobile units as separate factories, or components thereof, can present wearisome problems in describing condominium ownership. Assuming that such units are made part of the condominium real estate, even though they can be easily removed or altered, their description would be similar to stationary units. However, the underlying documents should provide for flexibility when needed changes are required in the future, but not to the detriment of other unit owners.

A mobile home compound for employees might be considered as part of a large-scale industrial condominium development. A mobile school complex could be part of a condominium ownership allied to an industrial area, a residential area, and perhaps additional commercial recreation complexes that service a community.

ADVANCED CONCEPTS IN CONSTRUCTION

Modern construction concepts may find wider use by way of condominium, even though begun on a traditional rental basis. Let us glance at use of property planned for a suburban warehouse park by a large retail department store that assembled the property for its own utilization consisting of approximately 500,000 square feet for warehousing. To make more intensive use of the 25-acre site, a three-story 1,350,000-square foot building, or vertical industrial park, is constructed. With the vertical format the building is equal in footage to a traditional horizontal park of approximately 90 acres. Trucks have direct access to loading and docking on each level because of unique construction techniques making the building conform to grade. Ceilings as high as 33 feet exist for convenience of larger vehicles.

If the condominium format were utilized, the cost of acquisition to the prime occupant could be substantially reduced by the sizeable purchase costs being borne by others, accompanied by relative convenience in independent ownership for all participants. Even if begun on a leasing basis, eventual conversion to condominium might liberate substantial investment capital, while retaining full ownership of the owner's prime space. If a high mortgage for the total property were available alternatively to the department store as a prime credit risk, the responsibility for the undertaking would mean a greater outlay of cash than if its financing involved only space actually used by the store in a condominium.

PROPERTY TAX ASSESSMENTS

It has already been indicated that condominium statutes generally require separate property tax assessments to be levied on the real property of each unit owner. Because of the newness of business condominiums, it can be expected that varying attitudes will be shown by assessors toward this problem. Sometimes the statute itself gives some guidelines for the assessor. For example, the New York statute states that: "In no event shall the aggregate of the assessment of the units plus their common interests exceed the total valuation of the property were the property assessed as a parcel."

In many cases, the assessors have first placed a total value on the entire condominium structure, then determined the tax burden per unit on the basis of the interests in the common elements attached to each unit. Sometimes this appears equitable, but at other times the procedure may be faulty, especially with the passage of time or when the initial percentage allocation was erroneous or unfair.

Residential condominium tax assessment procedures have often highlighted some of the rather arbitrary techniques in use in the property taxing field. This is especially the case when units of practically the same makeup and location are taxed differently. The general problems of this order will have to be faced by condominium owners just as in other situations involving property taxation. However, we can expect wider variations among commercial units in their initial cost, market value, and tax assessments.

Final strategies for tax assessment techniques have certainly not been set as yet, and considerable study and experience will be necessary to assure equitable treatment for unit owners and a fair sharing of the community tax burden placed on business and industry.

CHAPTER III

STRIDES IN BUSINESS OWNERSHIP OF REAL ESTATE

THE CONTINUING TREND FOR CHANGE

Before entirely or partially precluding other forms of business utilization of real estate in any situation, a look at underlying causes of current popular decisions would be helpful. Many unquestioned methods now in use came about through special demands brought on by emerging historical and economic factors peculiar to particular times that left longevity marks on many subsequent years of business real estate activities, well beyond memories of the causing institutions. Sometimes slow growth of a new method brought change, but most often, especially after the Civil War, sudden changes in industry components and public demand for products and services erupted into major new trends in business real estate techniques which tended to be long lasting.

The growing number of published histories of American businesses rarely probe this real estate aspect of American business development. Yet, real estate utilization has been a major portion of such living history. What changes are needed even now that will recast older segments of industry and direct new businesses for better efficiency of operations and public service?

As we examine the course of history from our special vista, we can see how events sometimes occurring within a short space of years helped form long-term habits until disrupted again by another series of sudden changes in business enterprise and demands. Short-term events forming long-term practice—this has been the more current history of business use of real estate. In the background are the historical threads of long-developed concepts, for example, the 400-year-old leasing arrangement as the rarely questioned chief alternative to ownership. Let us examine this total history now confronting the future of American business. By so doing, we also note the challenge of and to the business condominium concept.

LAND LEASES IN COLONIAL AMERICA

The word land*lord* may seem an anachronism in contemporary times, but its continued use demonstrates the strength and obviousness of its derivation. Most descriptively offensive words disappear with time, or are at the least recast to eliminate awkward or painful meanings of mere historical significance. Not this patronizing word. The medieval relationship of lord to vassal has, in most cases, been divested of feudal tributes and fealty to authority in the absolute sense; yet, courts, statutes, and contractual practice and tradition have carried over a considerable portion of the original distinction between landowner, or landlord, and those who must pay him for leave or license or freedom to use or enjoy his land and buildings.

In early America the land alone, with rare exception, provided the essential produce for the average man's income and livelihood. Many an immigrant unable to purchase land (much of which had been pre-empted by large estate holders through a royalty grant or bribery and corruption of officials) had to bond himself to a landlord, or *patroon*, to meet the requirements of succor. Others tilled the land under shorter-term agreements allowing participation in the crops, whence the word *cropper*. For those unable to purchase their own land, the degree of freedom or bondedness was usually determined by the fixed term of personal contractual obligation and limitations on wages, income, and selection and use of crops. Many workers could only purchase stores at landlord outlets, refine flour in his grist mills, and even entertain friends only during certain hours and days.

A great deal of the spirit to move westward was born of desire to escape the Eastern feudal patterns of land ownership. The ships that landed Europe's immigrants touched on land owned in huge tracts by chartered companies and the favored few who seized them through one device or another. The pack trains and wagons had to search in dangerous

Indian country for acreage to till in freedom from the outstretch of vast landlords, the settlers sometimes learning, to their chagrin, that they had selected land within the holdings of a landlord.

When arrangements to work the land were formally entered, they were sometimes referred to as *leases*. Leases were developed in England by 1500 to denote a recognized issuance of an interest in land somewhat protected by property law and comprising a grant of use and enjoyment of realty for, usually, a specified period under limitations of contractual obligations, the key one being the payment of money or kind periodically as *rent*. The distinguishing, though sometimes slim, difference between a mere labor agreement and a lease was protection against arbitrary landlord reentry in the latter case. Many such agricultural leases in Colonial America were for periods not exceeding a year at a time (the notable exception being almost indefinite small-plot leases in manorial vestiges in which "quitrents" began to serve in place of some services formerly performed for the lord and his family).

In some instances overall leases, typically for 99 years or other long terms, were arranged and finalized between royalty-backed companies and those fortunate few who were granted huge tracts in the new country, some the size of whole states. (Leases assigned to laborers were really subleases in such cases.) Although the long-term form of lease had no real connection to the farm-labor leases, both involved concepts important in the American history of leasing.

In a few instances perpetual or lifetime agricultural feudal arrangements lingered when legalities of manorial grants were continually upheld by officials and courts. Riots, strikes, and even murder spread throughout northeastern New York State because of the Van Rensselaer manorial remnants. In 1846 New York enacted constitutional amendments abolishing the feudal system and limiting agricultural leases to 12 years. The latter step began a trend among states to severely restrict the terms of agricultural leases. As we shall see, 50 years later this retarded the growth of industry in rural areas because the use of a long-term lease was unavailable as a financing device.

FACTORS RETARDING REALTY CONTROL BY COLONIAL INDUSTRY

A primary economic cause of divisiveness and dissension leading to the American Revolution was English regulatory restraint on native industry in the colonies. Although Napoleon derisively classified the English as a "nation of shopkeepers," the description may have been more appropriate for businesses in the American colonies. The Industrial Revolution began in England by the first decade of the nineteenth century—but not in the overseas colonies of the mother country. Royal strategy for colonial development in America was directed to the sale of new products of English industry or foreign products transported on English vessels. The net result of English prohibitions was extensive and painful smothering of substantial attempts to create competitive native American industry.

The greater part of American business became retail or wholesale shopkeeping or merchanting. The "merchants" usually were importers who owned a warehouse or "store" for goods handled in bulk, most selling both at wholesale and retail. Such latter real estate was often not part of a home residence, although sometimes it was attached or close by. Shopkeepers were usually retailers, typically residing in the same building as their shops and in many cases handling a variety or "general" merchandise. Specialization in colonial business was centered on the limited creative industries, such as blacksmithing, baking, or milling.

No zoning restrictions, in the modern sense, impeded the commercial use of homes, shops, or warehouses. One important business enterprise was without major real estate sedentary requirements, the growing peddling industry. Most such companies only needed strategically located warehouses to store their goods. These were mostly converted barns or buildings near wharves that accommodated shipping that refurbished supplies.

Some of the few attempts at industrial operations were limited by courts by way of common-law *nuisance* doctrines, especially products such as tallow candles and soap, whose manufacture occasionally putrified the air. The famous iron plantations in Pennsylvania were often self-contained villages spread over thousands of acres distant from other residential areas. In Hopewell Village, now a National Historic Site, the land was owned outright by the ironmasters, even though 99-year leases were used in many agricultural transactions in that colony and state.

Most retail and industrial enterprises during and soon after the American Revolution were housed in building structures providing high, bare walls and wide, bare floors, adequate for operation, easily rentable, and restorable on a short-term basis. Almost all equipment, shelving, and machinery were easily removable, with the problem of more substantial or awkwardly shaped equipment sometimes solved by placing it on open ground alongside the main building, as in the case of flour-grinding mills. Government itself also contributed some housing for business. A considerable number of central markets or fairs were organized by local governments at which stalls were rented to local merchants, mainly on a short-term basis. Again, operations could quickly be halted, equipment moved or dismantled, and the operator replaced.

Because of the largely unavailable privileged chartering of new corporations for ordinary businesses, most enterprises were operated as sole proprietorships or partnerships during the colonial years, with most larger businesses being run as partnerships. Almost half of the major business enterprises in Manhattan in the mid-eighteenth century were sole proprietorships. Because partnerships were easily dissolved by complaining partners or on the death of one participant, many businesses lacked the element of continuity essential for long-term stability.

In such an atmosphere of restraints on industry and short-term outlook, financing from whatever sources was also short term. Long-term mortgage financing for businesses just did not exist as a technique or even a concept, and for good reason when one considers the risks. The credit purchase of more extensive land and buildings customarily was by small down payment and yearly payment over a short term of interest and remaining debt to the seller. Many notes issued were callable at will and were the subject of bank discounting and rediscounting. Mortgages did not always accompany these transactions. Most businessmen, especially those not residing at their place of business, preferred short-term leasing arrangements, with the exception of larger enterprises needing major storage space tied to heavy shipping investment. An interesting industrial mortgage in 1793 involved the Hopewell iron forge properties in Pennsylvania, with the new owner, James Old, borrowing 8857 pounds, 14 shillings, and 5 pence from one Benjamin Morris, to be paid off in five annual installments, a transaction leading to foreclosure in 1800.

Additionally, the difficulties or impossibility in purchasing land held under long-term leases or outright by vast landowners further frustrated efforts to make long-term capital investments of the type required by promoters of major industry.

Those who controlled vast acreage or prime city property usually also held heavy investments in other enterprises, such as shipping and foreign trade. Depressions and panics and recessions in commercial trade arrived with continued frequency to plague those who controlled the land. First farmland acreage would be sold to pay debts arising elsewhere, then city land and buildings turned over for the same reasons, creating opportunities for purchase rather than short-term or long-term leasing, with a greater amount of immediate funds forthcoming to the owner from outright sale.

Curiously, at the same time that many sales were forced of valuable land in rural and city areas, continual immigration to the new country caused severe real estate shortages both for residential and commercial uses, imposing a fluctuating but regularly upward movement in land value even as sales had to be made to cure the debts of landowners. In a different banking system, there would have been much less turnover in land. But with the flimsy system in existence in the early nineteenth century in the United States, there was a constant movement with respect to land ownership.

Other factors aided in the mobility of land ownership during these years. Crown lands were taken by the new states and much of it marketed. Some states that initially protected excessively long-term leases, such as the famous 99-year variety, continually struck at these restraints on tenants by redemption legislation in aid of mobility in land ownership.

As the new nation emerged, commercial and industrial ventures in the first half of the nineteenth century were limited by the historical and traditional reliance on manufactures of other countries, poor transportation inland, a banking system not geared to finance long-term investment, difficulty in obtaining ownership of needed land as security for long-term planning, and inadequate forms of business enterprise for long-term ventures. It is not surprising that young American business did not often concern itself with long-term real estate acquisitions in that atmosphere.

PLANT SITES FOR INDUSTRY

Relieved from the choking of English rule, a new spirit of productive industry grew in many areas of the new states. The sites for most production were still the confines of the homes and lands of farmers and urban dwellers; family labor supplied the work effort. As we have noted, space requirements were not too difficult to satisfy for small or modest business productivity.

Larger enterprises were another matter.

Nineteenth century development of major industry in America was beset by two obstructive financial facts: the lack of long-term loan sources and the general public's and businessman's fear of debt. This may be hard to envision in our contemporary economy, whose very fabric is dependent on long-term real and personal property credit. But founding a new business 160 years ago could not presuppose long-term bank loans to enable purchase of land sites and construction of factories.

The shortest-period business debts are trade obligations on the sale of goods or credit, and these pulled shorter and shorter terms as the nineteenth century unfolded. The 6- to 12-month terms in 1800 dwindled to 4-month, then 90-day, and then 30–60-day expected payment by 1880. Although increased liquid capability from sale of goods arose from more swiftly efficient transportation and mail service, the shortening also emphasized the pressuring for cash self-financing from operations, as well as lack of faith in long-term debt obligations.

Newer large business enterprises usually were forced to purchase land and construct factories on a full cash outlay of capital funds. Extensions of existing businesses were likely to result from self-generated business funds or surplus.

Long-term-lease business obligations were not popular in the first two-thirds of the nineteenth century, probably because of the fear by landowners of the speculative dangers of new industries and the growing number of limited-use buildings and machinery required that might be difficult to sell, dismantle, or demolish if the occupant could not meet lease obligations. The concept of a lease being as good as the credit of a lessee was little espoused as basis for business decisions of much magnitude involving new industry, even though the "character" loan was often enough in agriculture. Widespread reports told that growing industries, such as steel, had to completely replace outdated machinery every 3 or 4 years. With the sudden awareness of perils from obsolescence of old and relatively new methods, factories, and machines, with the failures of businesses and banks in the many recessions and panics of the time, we can understand why prime landowners preferred immediate sales, or relatively short-term leases, rather than long-term leasing.

From the new industrialist's view, the long-term lease, although often not even available as a discussable alternative, would also be considered as pittable by abrasive elements. A sale or foreclosure on the owner's land might wipe out the lessee's interest. Temporary financial problems that made lease payments or other obligations impossible to meet could lead to a rapid termination of an entire business, for lease conditions and requirements in those years tended to be exceedingly onerous and restrictive. Moreover, the typical business mind of the time feared long-term debt of any sort.

The solution for new industry came from several directions, usually emphasizing full ownership of land and facilities. Such solutions probably helped postpone extensive use of long-term business leasing.

Counties, towns, and villages sometimes encouraged or promoted the founding of new industry by granting outright prime lands for such purposes, usually near natural power sources, such as a stream or river. Governments also authorized lotteries conducted by private business for development of new plants or expansion of plants, sites, and equipment. Additionally, more liberal corporation laws enacted by state legislatures aided industrial development by public subscription, although in earlier years special charters were still important. As an example important to American development of the textile industry, a water-edge site was purchased by a group including Francis C. Lowell in 1813 for the initiation of power loom production of cotton goods in Massachusetts, most of the funds coming from the sale of subscriptions authorized by the charter of incorporation specially and wisely issued by the state of Massachusetts.

By such techniques in financing, many larger entrepreneurs grasped the growing number of business opportunities created by new inventions and power sources and changing public demand. But let it not be assumed that new or old enterprises had it easy when it came to "going public" for funds. Banks, railroads, and public utilities could sell their shares publicly with some success, but until the 1880s very few enterprises in the industrial category could succeed in financing this way, probably for the same reasons that landowners distrusted the reliability of newcomers. A large percentage of corporate financing originated in Europe. As painful as it may sound, most American industrial enterprises until that time expanded through mere reinvestment of earnings. Most of those who could not raise adequate funds this way stayed small or perished along the way by inability to compete efficiently; some were occasionally tided over by short-term or demand loans from private professional lenders or banks. Stores of savings in banks and other institutions did not exist as a formidable factor in the real estate market in the United States until the next century with the growth of long-term depositories that began to feed the mortgage market.

To the 1880s larger business production facilities, especially those specializing in new products and recently invented techniques and machinery, could most typically be found located on self-owned property. If leases were involved in operations, they were customarily for smaller ventures and short term. The commercial districts of Chicago and Detroit, for example, show a negligible number of business property leases beyond 20-year terms recorded until 1890. (State laws permitting or requiring recordation of long-term leases for title clarification purposes are largely responsible for this important historical information.)

We come to 1890 with, mainly, two forms of long-term ground leases in vogue in a few areas: the familial 99-year or lesser-term lease kept or renewed from former days, remaining from those who had not been eliminated or spun off by legislation or hard times; and the home and farm financing device in a few states, notably Ohio and Pennsylvania, involving long-term ground rents, usually on existing land and improvements with the direct or implicit right of the lessee to construct necessary farm or home quarters. This latter type lease could not be entered in many other states because, as we have noted, they barred agricultural leases beyond a few years. The Maryland 99-year lease must be reviewed separately because it had distinguishing features which we discuss below. Nevertheless, events were proceeding in the spreading cities that would soon bring the long-term commercial lease into much wider use.

THE NEW LONG-TERM LEASE: CONSTRUCTION BY LESSEE

Beginning around 1900 a new type of long-term lease began to be used in the promotion of new business ventures, especially in growing urban areas.

Until that time, as we have seen, the long-term lease was occasionally used in the United States, but not customarily in business ventures. (For purposes of discussion we consider long-term leases as those in excess of 20 years.) In addition, it was rare that construction by the lessee of specific improvements existed as a required condition of a lease. The major exception, and forerunner of a new trend, was the Maryland 99-year lease. The terms and reasons for such lease in that state are thoroughly described in a court decision (*Banks* v. *Haskie*, 45 Maryland 207) in which Judge Miller, writing in a case before the Maryland Court of Appeals involving a 99-year lease with terms for perpetual renewal stated:

"The owner of vacant ground in a town located and about to be built up, from which he can derive in its then condition no adequate income, being himself unable or unwilling to erect the necessary buildings, instead of selling the property in fee for its then value and investing the proceeds in other securities, or raising by mortgage the money to make the improvements himself, resorts to this method of deriving an income from it, and making a secure and permanent investment of its value in the land itself. He makes a lease of it by which he secures the erection of improvements, which enhance the value of his property, and consequently make a permanent and safe investment of its actual market value, and this is all he had in view or intended to accomplish. The lessee is encouraged to spend his money in improvements by the permanency of the interest he acquires, and expectation of further increase in value, which will enable him also to realize a profit from the expenditure of his means. Thus a mutual advantage was contemplated by both parties at the time, and the result has usually been beneficial to both. Such appears to us to be the intention and purpose of the parties in making and accepting a lease of this description, and the Courts should so treat and construe the instrument as most effectually to carry out that intent. This character of tenure is, so far as we know, among the States peculiar to Maryland. It has not been generally adopted so far as we are informed in any other State. It was introduced here in Colonial times, and has been a favorite system of tenure from a very early period. A large city has been built, and improved, and a vast majority of the real estate in Baltimore is now held under it. It is not open to any of the objections against perpetuities. * * * these leasehold interests devolve upon the personal representatives of the owner, are in terms made assignable, and they, as well as the ownerships in fee under the denomination of 'ground rents,' are subjects of daily transfer, and are constantly sought for as safe investments of capital. It is a peculiar description of tenure which has been sustained by our Courts, and approved and fostered by our people. While the ground rents from their nature are usually of a fixed value, the leasehold interests are more or less fluctuating. In many, and indeed in most cases, they have largely increased in value with the growth of the city. And most extensive and costly improvements have been and are daily made by owners of such interests on grounds thus leased."

It is quite possible that one reason the early DuPonts purchased sites in Delaware, rather than in more industrialized Maryland, was the desire to own land outright rather than under Maryland leases.

THE NEED FOR THE NEW-FORM LONG-TERM LEASE

Rampant growth of American commerce by 1890 was fed by industrialization. Self-contained home industry and nonmechanized commercial activity were declining rapidly. Huge enterprises developed throughout the United States corralling substantial monopolies in various businesses such as in steel and oil refining. Small- and middle-sized firms began to grow for the purposes of servicing and tooling larger companies. Mass production meant more intensive marketing procedures and advertising methods that concomitantly demanded prime business space in leading cities.

Scarcity in a land containing vast open spaces evolved. New industry had to be located near the homes of workers, although sometimes homes for industrial workers were constructed under auspices of the new manufacturing plants. Outlying agricultural lands were ordinarily not available for manufacturing or industrial purposes because of difficulty in purchase and statutes barring long-term leases on such land, as we have seen. (In many instances if promoters of industry were to have made representations of nonagricultural use of property rimming the cities to farmers it would have resulted in untenable pricing of the land.) More important, the requirements of larger and more specialized work forces for small- and middle-sized companies necessitated location near residence concentrations as well as transportation hubs to receive raw materials and new fuels and to ship out finished products, which meant the growing cities.

Looking about for a financing device to aid in production of new commercial and industrial facilities, businessmen began to settle on the Maryland type of long-term lease as a financing device. This was so because of the need for the lessee to be able to construct a facility for production with the security of long-term use of premises and improvements, without having to pay immediately for urban land which was beginning to skyrocket in price.

On the other hand, most large industries at this time owned the land on which their plants or offices were located, or purchased such assets shortly after business began to expand. The Maryland type of lease, which ordinarily involved perpetual renewals, after a while was only a remote cousin to the new forms of leasing that land owners and speculators evolved with the growing commercial and industrial group in urban communities. The Maryland lease, as seen from the foregoing case, was originally renewable perpetually, eliminating the worry of reversions to the landowner. Moreover, its terms before renewability usually involved a 99-year period at a fixed annual rent. In addition, the Maryland leases had been negotiated mostly at times when land was relatively cheap, with the ground rent not a major problem with respect to the burden of payments. The Maryland system was based on a tradition originated by the founders of that colony whereby most land ownership was by long-term lease, with little need for outright purchase of a fee by farmer or urban dweller because of the perpetual renewal clause.

Use of the long-term lease for the acquisition of a business site was striking in its popularity in some cities. Just prior to World War II, one out of two business buildings in downtown Chicago was under long-term lease, many for 99 years. Prior to 1890 very few leases had been recorded in that city. In most cities large numbers of leases did not run as long as 99 years, with each business area developing its own standard term. For example, in New York State the 21-year lease was typical. Many of the leases in Detroit and Chicago ran for approximately 50 years. Most commercial land leases in urban areas were not perpetually renewable, and often included terms considerably different from the Maryland fixed-rent formula, especially with the passage of years. In some cases rents were automatically increased at the end of short-term interim periods such as 3, 5, or 10 years. Later, the "percentage" lease came into use, tying income factors to rent.

The benefit of so-called "100 percent land financing" by long-term leases came about in a marketplace in which the emerging banking system initially did not ordinarily provide long-term mortgage loans that blanketed construction and permanent financing. Short-term balloon-type mortgages made this type of financing perilous, in contrast to the security from small, regular payments required by leasing. The Hopewell ironworks mortgage of 1800, with its 5-year maturity, differed little from private or bank business-property mortgages 100 years later.

In effect, the new small- and middle-sized business ventures often found little alternative to leasing for promotion of a new business in an urban area. This problem was accentuated by another factor impeding full ownership of land: the insistence of many of the long-time landowners in retaining land in their families rather than permitting sale of their holdings, even if the switch to business use was contemplated. The only alternative in the latter case in certain areas was the ground lease, even for larger enterprises. A somewhat parallel situation has faced new industry seeking land purchases in fast-urbanizing Hawaii in the past few years. That state has developed considerably by use, much more generally than in other areas of the United States, of long-term leases in the past 20 years.

TWENTIETH CENTURY PATTERNS OF REALTY HOLDINGS

Three concepts underlying business realty holdings have dominated transactional development since 1900, with a fourth factor, income taxation, emerging to condition and even override the other three. Those three elements are

1. Acceptance of long-term investment in business sites by industrial companies for manufacturing and office purposes.
2. Acceptance by business of real estate terms and transactions permitting the landlord or other parties direct or indirect participation in business earnings.
3. Pressures for favorable financial reporting techniques by publicly held companies.

As we analyze these factors, noting their derivation, history, and validity, we also evaluate whether the business condominium alternative is now more apt for many current and future business real estate solutions, especially amid the growth of American depositories of huge savings, such as banks and insurance companies, that provide mortgage funds.

FULL OWNERSHIP OR LONGER LEASES

Even as industry searched to meet fiercely growing competition and gobbling giants, the quest for business sites necessitated longer vistas for planning. The typical short-term nineteenth century lease of 1 to 3 years grew after 1900 to 10-year periods in many cases, with an average of 5 years. Businesses became more complex, and land-value upsurges tipped the scale in favor of more permanent decisions because of greater difficulties in moving expensive equipment amid expected rising rentals.

The shorter a lease term, the more profit sharing in nature the agreement is. On each occasion for renewal, the profitability factor is considered by the landlord. In addition, the competition for space by other businesses can pressure rentals upward, even if a resident business has not increased sales measurably. Thus the more major the enterprise, the more major the expenditures for capital site and building construction and improvements, and the greater the value built from emphasizing particular location, the larger is the need for protection from unknown contingencies flowing from short-term rentals.

If financing devices of the time had provided adequate means for land acquisition, many newer and middle-sized companies would have avoided short- or long-term leasing. With limited institutional and noninstitutional help for longer-term venture capital, the landlord and entrepreneur had to literally create financing devices much by themselves.

With the great resourcefulness of acquisitive companies following the monopoly trail, business dealings became imbued with the idea that larger buyers should get better pricing. To exist, many companies had to seek more and more outlets for manufacturing and marketing, in order to stay alive by large-scale purchasing. This fact necessitated branching businesses into many new locations, with the accompanying problem of financing new sites. For this reason, even some of the larger firms in the early twentieth century used the long-term lease as a part of overall operating technique.

If long-term mortgages on business property had been available, many long-term leases would not have existed. Until the late 1940s commercial banks and insurance companies were greatly restricted by state and federal regulations from making loans on business property, emphasizing residential realty as the backbone of their realty lending practices. However, corporations did make substantial realty acquisition for business operations from the sale of their own equity and debenture securities, the investment banking industry opening wide to embrace growing American industry.

The long-term lease, in the interim, made good sense in many instances for the following reasons:

1. Because of the need for heavy investment in plant and machinery, the use of land without purchase cut immediate burdens on initial expenditures.

2. Payments for land were spread out over long terms: terms of 21, 50, even 99 years.

3. Skyrocketing land prices sometimes made it impossible to purchase land, even if considered desirable.

4. Some landholders stubbornly refused to sell their land, especially in valuable downtown areas of growing cities.

5. In some cases, the landowner required continued operation of his own property, although with limited use that permitted leasing for other utilization. For this reason, valuable air space was leased by railroads in Chicago and New York for overhead construction of investment realty.

LESSOR PARTICIPATION IN BUSINESS PROFITS

With the burgeoning growth of American business in the early twentieth century, landowners endeavored to inject profit capability in long-term leases so that they could share in increased lessee earnings. This was accomplished in several ways: clauses permitting periodic increases in rental amounts, net or gross profit-sharing leases, escalation clauses to ward off increased expenses that would dilute rental income, and other devices peculiar to different decades.

After World War II it was not uncommon for a substantial sum to be paid in advance to the lessor for a guaranteed-constant, ground-rent lease, apparently to keep the landowner's claws out of future profits. This format was sometimes used even though the lessee had formidable obligations for construction or improvements, although it was more usual for existing properties.

A WORD ABOUT LEASEHOLD MORTGAGES

The concept of issuing mortgage loans secured by only the tenant's interest was considered highly speculative and unpopular for many years by ordinary lending sources, especially when a fee mortgage already existed. The danger of a security wipeout from tenant default was just too trying a thought for lenders until the 1920s, when they let their caution out to the winds. Most such leasehold mortgages, when issued, were the subject of investment or bond company public issues, often by splitting the mortgage bonds into small segments. Although total real estate bond issues, including substantial leasehold obligations (even second, third, and fourth obligations) were around $150,000,000 in 1913, the amount jumped to $5,040,000,000 by 1930. S. W. Straus and Company, for example, by 1926 the largest such dealer in the United States, in 1898 had adopted the plan of splitting up each mortgage into a series of bonds to sell to many investors, instead of one, in small denominations such as $100 or $500. That company, until 1926, dealt principally in first-mortgage real estate bonds, including business properties. It then proceeded to perform the same function with bonds covering leasehold mortgages. By February 1931 the firm could not meet its obligations to bondholders. The effect of such failure, as with similar firms, heightened business difficulties in financing by mortgaging leases thereafter.

For approximately 15 years the situation remained constant in limited use of leasehold mortgage financing, until more contemporary realty financing took a new turn after World War II. However, just as the Maryland leases were only remote cousins of later long-term leases, so with later forms of leasehold mortgages when compared with the 1926 variety, as we shall see.

Long-term leases were forced into the flow of commerce by economically justified financing factors in 1900. But the surge of leaseholds and their financing in the 1920s was another matter. In too-numerous instances buildings were transferred or constructed on a long-term leasehold basis more for the purpose of selling bonds than for needs of operating businesses. Leaseholds, subleaseholds, and subsubleaseholds were engineered by speculators, with bonds sold to cover each level of the pyramid. Office buildings, rather than industrial plants, were the prime targets.

THE DECLINE IN LEASING (1932–1940)

From 1932 to 1940 the long-term lease declined in use, probably because of the lack of long-term confidence in business in general and the drying up of interest in new plants and industries. In addition, financing by leasehold mortgages became an ominous device, rarely utilized in substantial ventures because of the fresh memory of the hordes of such mortgages wiped out.

A KEY REMNANT OF LONG-TERM LEASING: PERCENTAGE LEASES

Before we move to more recent times in our discussion and confront realty decisions with the business condominium, we should review the percentage lease concept and its development from 1900 to the end of World War II. It was born out of the long-term lease, without which it would never have been possible. The percentage concept, which later gave rise to sale-leaseback and mortgagee equity participations, forbodes the future need for the business condominium as an alternative to modern forms of long-term leasing.

THE PERCENTAGE LEASE: FIRST USED WITH CHAIN STORES

The growth of chain stores in the United States had been slow in the first decade and a half into the 1900s; most expansion had come from reinvestment of profits. Beginnnng about 1915, the expansion formula adopted the long-term lease, but it was different on two scores from the leases that came into wide vogue in 1900. The chain store lessee did not build his own premises; the landowner constructed the improvement. The rent was variable, based on a percentage of sales or earnings.

It would appear that the popularity of long-term, constant-payment leases had been affected by landowner awareness that such undertakings removed the lessor from participation in growing land values. What had appeared as a windfall in 1900 began to look like a landowner's folly 15 years later. By 1915, more than 30 percent of industry was electrified and nearly 11 million telephones were in use, ten times the number in 1900. More and more intensive use and profitability was exacted from business use of land, with the growing number of skyscrapers revolutionizing land use.

In this atmosphere, the landowner in downtown districts often sought a future-increment factor in any lengthy lease. In the case of chain stores, a landowner did not mind constructing stores with his own or bank funds, so long as he could participate in future profitability.

As shall be seen, we are still in the landlord-participation phase of business ownership begun by chain stores in 1915, although the refinements added to the percentage concept have been amazing.

PERCENTAGES WITHIN DIVIDED SPACE: DEPARTMENTS WITHIN STORES

Percentage rentals were not typical of substantial business leases until the end of World War II. Prior to then, most frequently the concept was utilized, in addition to chain stores, in rented departmental divisions of department stores. The compelling factors making business tenants yield appeared to be the attractive uniqueness of newly constructed or modernized business locations and the growing search for prestige sites in downtown areas.

Internal control capability made the department store tenants considerably more accountable for sales and profits than ordinarily possible. Unlike the national chain store, often publicly held and keeping careful records, the average tenant in most other situations fought lease terms, or their implementation, whenever outside examination of sales and income were at issue. Without reliability of such procedures to accurately reflect actual sales and income, the percentage method was a hive of stinging problems.

In most cases, percentage rentals only began after payment of an agreed minimum rental base. During the Depression, some tenants insisted on straight-percentage leases, so that hard times would not exacerbate inability to pay even minimum rentals.

Doubtlessly many smaller- and middle-sized business enterprises, from the earliest days of the use of percentage rentals, had to bypass opportunities for prime locations because of their refusal to yield their privacy in business operations to such lease terms, or because lessors were dubious of the reliability of tenants to maintain adequate, auditable records.

OFFICE SKYSCRAPERS AND PERCENTAGE LEASES

One of the newest forms of business structure, the skyscraper office buildings, had largely to disregard the percentage concept because many tenants kept only offices or showrooms that were a small area of overall realty occupancy rather than self-contained businesses measurable by incoming and outgoing inventories. In this situation, other devices for income participation have been used. Initially skyscraper leases typically contained automatic increases in rentals on a periodic basis, irrespective of future economic or business conditions. Such terms were often entered into with little knowledge of business growth capability, by lessee or lessor, but they did enable immediate occupancy for tenants in the majestic structures pointing skyward.

Landlords were not deterred fully in their quest for income participation from office rentals. Short renewal terms were set with regular increases in rent. With the initial or automatically increased rental as a starting point, later clauses began to appear, especially after World War II, tying additional rent increases to such price indices as the *Wholesale Price Index* published by the U.S. Department of Commerce, and the *Consumer Price Index* published by the Bureau of Labor Statistics. Although percentage rentals are tied to *actual* profitability, such indices may or may not have relevance to a particular business. Nevertheless, practicality made alternatives impossible in many situations. Space shortages in some prestige office building locations after 1945 created a lessor's market that incorporated new index devices such as these for sharing in future profitability, implicitly assuming that expected inflation and profitability were coextensive.

Although major industries owned plant and production facilities, the practicality for ownership of prestige office and marketing space was just not available in a large number of instances.

PERCENTAGE LEASES HAVE OVERTAKEN RETAIL MARKETS

In recent years, major retail store expansion by lease arrangements has been almost exclusively by percentage rent agreements, typified by the modern huge suburban shopping centers which have been replacing traditional downtown centers.

It will aid us considerably in evaluating the commercial condominium alternative to examine the growing pains that were occasioned while this profit-sharing method of controlling valuable space was taking shape. Three factors mainly contributed to blocking the widespread use of percentage lease clauses before the end of World War II.

1. Hesitancy by tenants to submit to periodic audits and other restrictive conditions.

2. Slow growth of accounting standards: internal and external auditing.

3. Competition from landowners offering other participation techniques considered less onerous to lessees.

GROUND LEASE RENT VARIATIONS

In addition to the variations resulting from income percentage rent formulas, contractual provisions in ground leases can also divert increased company profitability to rent payments.

The term *ground lease* long ago became traditional to describe the right to use land as if vacant or detachable from property improvements, as distinguished from a combination lease that incorporates both land and improvements without regard for the physical severance of permanent land and depreciable buildings and other improvements. Ground leases, as we have seen, were originally for vacant land, sometimes with rights of use or construction obligatory or discretionary for the lessee. Formerly, when a landlord leased land with the requirement that he construct lessee facilities, it was usually conceived as a combination lease. In modern times, however, interesting pie-cutting financing devices have been conceived that have dissolved the combination of land and existing improvements, using the slices for varying degrees of profitability. To distinguish that part of real property retained or cut out of the fee made up of land, the ancient term *ground lease* has been reincarnated.

It is customary to include a continuing rental reevaluation clause in modern ground leases, usually based on a percentage of periodically reappraised value. Thus the ground lease itself becomes an income participation vehicle, because in the overwhelming number of cases it is the increasing productivity of the lessee's operations that up the appraisal of land value. Indeed, the large number of court cases reported in Illinois, California, Maryland, and New York show the modern ground lease to be a highly litigious concept—especially with rental reevaluation clauses.

In effect, contemporary ground leasing is another method of income participation by the nonoperating, often passive, landowner. It is now not unusual for him to subordinate his position to achieve the desired end result, assigning away the mortgagability of his interest in return for obtaining the long-term participation leasehold.

Along the way in this form of relationship, the landowner might separately lease land and improvements, or a subagreement might be entered between a third party investor and the original owner, or a dozen other cutups of leasing arrangements take place, which remove the directness of landlord-tenant relationships and create more than one nonoperating party eagerly seeking participations in profits. For such reasons, lease renegotiation is sometimes surprisingly difficult for the operating tenant on expiration of term, or when business problems occur making continued operations onerous.

Although writers continue to justify ground leases for the long-ago reasons of being economic devices to save the cost of land purchase, this factor is often only the initiating device for direct profit-sharing arrangements. As such, the concept is consistent with modern leasing assumptions that continually reduce the independence of operating business management.

After World War II, some economic theorists supported long-term leasing on the basis of prior success with reducing immediate needs for venture capital. Why pay in full for land now when you only want to use part of its services? But, unforetold by such theorists, was the continual diminution of independent management accompanying many leases.

Looking back historically, we noted the salient features of the 99-year and other long-term leases prior to World War II. They appear to have served the needs for different periods for reasons stated.

Whatever the necessity for retention of the old forms with new income-sharing provisions, there is equally the need to eliminate pressures on independence and profitability. Originally, financing problems often mandated ground rent arrangements. Reaction to oppressive conditions in this area now is ample reason for a revolutionary new concept—the business condominium. The ownership of merely an undivided interest in land removes some of the burdens of purchasing, perhaps, in many instances, a small price for demolishing contemporary profit-sharing procedures.

Today large initial cash payments for obtaining lucrative leases are not unusual burdens for lessees. In the early years after World War II, and in a few current instances, such an early lump payment bought off future profit terms in leases. As time has progressed, however, lessors of prime properties have more and more demanded both large lump payments for leases as well as provisions for profit participation. Additionally, resale and reassignment of leases by lessees to others also carry lump sum plus profitability terms. Sometimes the purchasers are operating firms; in other cases purchasers for investment only. In the maelstrom of such activity, the ground lessor may condition approval of such transactions on a more substantial inroad on profits from resale, operations, refinancing, or similar directions. Quite often such payments are a direct contradiction to the cost-saving argument originally surrounding the ground lease. The landowner gets a large slice of cake to eat, a fat chunk of sales value plus a participation interest in profits. Custom has made such practice widespread, with tax factors adding fuel. The owner receives less immediate income than by outright sale, and can become a partner to growth in an operating business by percentage and reevaluation clauses.

Faced with this growing custom in real estate, the lessee should welcome consideration of new techniques strengthening his hold on his own profits and removing him from the vagaries of a lessee and coventurer status. Foremost in such evaluation should be the business condominium.

LENDER PARTICIPATIONS

Various pressures on institutional lenders in the past few years have helped change their basic motivations from simple construction and permanent financing of loan arrangements to equity participations and similar devices for sharing in profitability. When one considers the forces at work on lending institutions, it can be foreseen that such pressures will be prevalent factors whenever market forces permit. Some of these reasons have been and will be

1. The growing impositions on institutions by federal and state income tax legislation.
2. Greater depositor demands for higher rates of return on deposits and bank securities.
3. The instability and declines in availability of adequate sources of revenue from traditional investments.
4. The need by publicly held commercial banks to show increased earnings in reports that are publicly distributed to stockholders at regular intervals.

In the past few years the lending institutions have striven in several directions to enlarge the possibilities for profiting from operational real estate business enterprises. In addition to a host of new financing techniques tied to conventional loan-interest procedures and the derivation of allied income, there has been a definite trend to share in an equity position and thereby profit directly from operation of investment properties by borrowers seeking financing. Indeed, professional financing advisory firms have come into existence recently, specializing in the marriage between institutions and developers that is founded on equity participation by both parties. In some instances several institutions have even syndicated real estate purchases without noninstitutional partners.

Generally there have been two avenues for institutional participation.

In one case the lender overtly seeks direct and current operational income tied to immediate day-to-day business functioning by an operating business. Often, however, the institution is passive in its approach to day-to-day management decisions, perhaps limited by fear of violation of existing banking laws or Treasury requirements, as in the case of real estate investment trusts. The latter attitude is often only a smokescreen for real control, which is afforded by those who hold the reins on overall policy decisions. For example, devices are used such as the power to name one or more board members or to veto certain key policy decisions. This type of direct participation is exemplified by arrangements for institutional sharing in a percentage of gross or net income or cash flow from operations, sometimes tied to a formula changing participation based on sales growth. The other, and often combined, method of participation by institutions emphasizes contingent production of additional income in later periods for the institution. For example, into this category come arrangements for sharing capital profits on later sales of valuable real estate, rights to percentage income from new or expanded facilities in later years, valuable stock options or other preferences in connection with future public or private financing, as well as other imaginative formulas which have been used to the present time or which will be concocted in the future. In some cases in which the borrower will receive rental income from others, insurance companies provide for sharing in future increases at a specific rate, such as 20 percent.

In effect, by these devices the lender becomes a current or contingent partner in an operational business enterprise. It is true that he requires his extended position into operational lucre in many situations because, he defends, the institution has made an enormous investment of its lending capacity for which mere interest on the loan is not adequate. The "kickers" are also a means for avoiding the psychological embarrassment of mathematical computation of real return to the institution for its loan or investment. And, it should be pointed out, there have been many occasions when the equity participation comes free to the bank of an equity investment. Although in some states usury statutes present problems, it is doubtful that such obstruction will be long lasting amid the continuing demands for greater growth in American industry. Moreover, there is a definite trend in the country to limit usury statutes to individual rather than corporate borrowers.

Thus American business is directly confronted with the growing inroads of institutional control and even domination in the future as the price to be paid for heavy borrowing to finance industry, especially for real estate development which is traditionally operated under a financing plan in which institutional lenders post the highest degree of investment funds and the developer has traditionally invested only a small amount of overall capital requirements. When one reflects on the enormity of institutional participations, it is to be expected that a greater share of the pie will be sought.

The business condominium form, in contradiction to lender participation situations, can through syndication by a group of unit owners cut down the needs for institutional aid in capital formations. When possible, the use of several rather than a single lending institution can automatically remove the problem because no single, huge, permanent loan is required, even though the total of all the loans may be the equivalent of an overall one.

It is also possible that in the future no business loans for real property development will be free of some sort of equity participation, but the business condominium format may still lessen the impact on the profitability of a single borrower resulting from institutional pressures for equity participation.

The business condominium can, therefore, help to forestall the growing power of institutional lenders in American business and help provide greater opportunities for the operational activities of business to be free of outside influences frustrating continuing freedom of choice.

JOINT VENTURING BY CONDOMINIUM

Most real estate joint ventures and syndicates in the 1970s have been passive in nature. That is to say, in most instances investors have pooled funds to create or obtain ownership of valuable real estate properties for the purpose of profiting from income paid by lessees and other operators for use of the premises. In only an insignificant number of cases, rarely involving larger properties, have operating businesses syndicated the acquisition of real estate for the direct utilization of the premises by a pooled arrangement.

The business condominium may radically change the accepted system of joint venturing and syndication. Businesses would pool acquisition costs and resources for the joint operation of self-owned property. To date, larger corporations have occasionally pooled together by the creation of single subsidiary corporation controlled jointly by the parent firms, in which the product involved was necessary to meet joint requirements. However, this type of subsidiary corporation is really a single form of enterprise in its day-to-day business activities, subject to joint control by the outside corporations. The business condominium, on the other hand, makes it possible for several businesses to operate directly and independently at the same premises without the control or domination of one by the other. By the business condominium device syndication and joint-venturing opportunities can be shared by the operating companies themselves, thus eliminating the middleman profits of passive real estate investors. The host of incremental rent terms and profit sharing by passive owners would be eliminated.

The business condominium also offers the opportunity for passive investors to purchase portions of commercial buildings for investment, even though they otherwise would be foreclosed by lack of funds or the risk if the only alternative was the total purchase of a valuable property. In addition, the passive condominium owner can depend less on absentee control by a general partner of a real estate syndication, because the business condominium format permits independent ownership of divided space together with a constant voice in policy management of commonly used areas. This greater freedom to the passive investor is largely unobtainable by the use of traditional, limited partnership formats. In this connection the business condominium, in many situations, is a far superior vehicle for investment.

It is also quite possible, as in South America, for ownership of different spaces in business condominiums to be divided among passive and operational owners. Thus an office building with eight floors can be owned by eight different condominium units owners, four of whom use the premises themselves. Or, as was done in Boston recently, a major tenant can purchase as a condominium unit the office building space in which it had already satisfactorily established its residence in a third of the building. The degree of flexibility for arrangements in this type of situation is enormous. Among the benefits of such flexibility are more accurate cost planning and the greater ease in removal from premises, with even a substantial profit, as against the operator of a business faced with the problems of breaking a long-term lease.

BALANCE SHEET AND PROFIT PRESENTATIONS

The popularity of new public issues of securities since the end of World War II has encouraged many companies to "go public" by selling once privately held firms to public investors through issuance of equity securities. In many cases the offerings of stock do not involve much in new additions of capital to the issuing companies, but rather are liquidations of partial equity ownership by controlling parties. In other instances, especially untried enterprises, funds may be directed to new activities of young companies. In almost all cases a dominant determining force for the issuance of securities to the public is the promoter's quest for capital gains tax treatment for proceeds coming from such procedure.

Concomitant with such an issuance of securities is the obligation thenceforward to issue financial statements, such as balance sheets and profit-and-loss statements to investors. Moreover, companies that have traveled the public route previously, even the so-called "blue chip" issues listed on national stock exchanges, are continually posed with the problem of presentation of the financial condition of their companies. Accounting for debt obligations is thus an important feature to be considered by publicly held companies that wish to market or remarket securities. In addition, the balance sheets of all companies, even those not publicly held, are of consequence with respect to lines of credit for the conduct of business or for similar purposes.

A curious accounting deception has become legally permissible by custom and even an avowed viewpoint of the accounting profession. Substantial lease obligations by lessees need not be stated in the debt obligation portion of corporate balance sheets. In the usual case, at most, such obligations are merely footnoted, even though the debt is firm and is as much a contracted obligation as a note payable. The magic word "lease" shelters the debt obligation from the debt portion of the balance sheet. On the other hand a straight-mortgage type of obligation typical in real estate dealings must be included directly in the obligation portion of the balance sheet.

For the aforesaid reasons, financial advisors have sometimes favored lease positions for their client over the outright purchase of real estate. In modern times, leasing contrivances for real property have been fanatically pursued to secure maximum benefits from balance sheet presentation as well as use of valuable property. Just as importantly, the reports of profits to American stockholders have become shrunken, alum-fed concoctions of costs leaned against a fattened exposition of profit. It is the current and future true profit picture that may sometimes win the day for the business condominium over leasing arrangements. Business condominiums require less mortgaging for individual purchasers than would be the case if the total property were acquired by the same participant, and after all, leasehold mortgages of larger amounts might be required of lessees. Sometimes the larger freedom to employ space by condominium owners can bring greater profit in later periods without the penalties that often attend changes in the use of premises under expensive leases. Acceleration of depreciation write-offs accompanies the business condominium purchaser as the buyer and owner of real estate, thus sheltering mortgage cost. In addition, such expensive items as transportation costs can sometimes be cut by the convenient proximity of suppliers or buyers occasioned by the location of the condominium. This could also occur if such conveniences as water supply, airports, and railroad sidings are well located near the condominium building. In addition, joint use of expensive equipment can give rise to substantial efficiencies that further reduce costs. Careful planning might very well reduce the wasting of space, provide more flexibility in operations, and derive the efficiencies attending good location and joint operations where feasible.

If, then, the condominium purchaser is not able to project a lowered debt on his balance sheet, he may well be able to cut his costs and produce more profits. The profit-and-loss part of financial statements must therefore be thoroughly explored in evaluating public projections of changes in financial condition.

Every business venture is a different one, and no general rule can be applicable to all companies. Hasty conclusions about balance sheet presentations should not impede thorough evaluation of business condominium profitability factors.

TAX HISTORY AND REAL ESTATE USE

In studying, through historical perspective, the modern rationale for use of real property in commerce, we have thus far emphasized such distinguishing features as the incidence of allowable control by investors of their own business operations and the growing problems in dilution of profitability stemming from *owner* versus *user* relationships. But we must also consider incursions on cash flow by income tax factors and what the effects of choice of methods in the use of land and buildings and other improvements are, especially when considering the business condominium versus leasehold arrangements.

Income tax problems must be viewed against contemporary history, because they were of little or no significance amid the growth and development of most of the traditional and even the more modern real estate concepts whose history we have probed.

The United States enacted its first personal income tax law on August 5, 1861. Some European countries, notably England, Austria, and Italy had already captured revenue from such tax source by that time. In 1895, a then-extant income tax measure was declared unconstitutional by the United States Supreme Court. Apparently unshielded by the decision, corporations were placed under a separate tax on net income in 1909. The 1913 final ratification of the 16th amendment led to package enactments covering both individuals and business entities in the search for new federal revenues in single legislation.

Although initially income tax levies were minimal, Congress soon jumped on the tax to replace the prior dependence for revenue on excise taxes. A mere 7 percent was the maximum personal income tax rate for the years 1913 to 1915, but was increased to a whopping 77 percent by 1918, along somewhat progressive rates. Corporate income, which had been taxed at only 1 percent from 1913 to 1915, rose to 12 percent by 1918. By 1920, two-thirds of national tax revenue was derived from the income tax on business and individuals.

Economic and war emergencies later led to steeper rates and wider population coverage. Today the typical American businessman, side by side with his financial and legal advisors, probably spends more time trying to avoid taxes than on any other planning function in his business. So, too, are the problems posed in handling acquisition of real estate use by full ownership or under leases.

It is not unusual for commercial condominium developers to set up promotional tables of projected figures comparing the real costs between use of the building involved by lease or by condominium, with important reference to tax aspects. Each venture is unique, as are the tax aspects. For example, the benefits of available fast depreciation of building improvements by a unit owner must be judged against possible amortization of total leasehold cost (land and building). Land is not depreciable for income tax purposes, and thus its cost to a full owner cannot be quickly retrieved by a tax write-off of cost, as is the case for the building and improvements. On the other hand, all rentals are usually deductible, even for use of land; initial costs to procure leasehold positions can often be written off as constant amortization costs on income tax returns even though they involve payment for use of land. This inconsistency in allowing write-offs for land costs often gives rise to arguments that it can be more favorable, tax-wise, to lease rather than to own.

In some situations, developers frustrated by this different treatment of land cost have tried to adjust the difference artificially in dangerous ways. For example, in trying to encourage a preference for condominium, a developer may fabricate some hypothetical wizardry such as "annual appreciation gain," to achieve a mathematical result on a projection table. To show some sort of appreciation in condominium unit value yearly, such as the popular "5 percent," requires quite a bit of dreaming and does not belong on a cost-income table, irrespective of the likelihood of inflation or shortage of similar properties in the future.

Developers who yield to the easy thinking of such questionable strategies as above sometimes overlook sales analysis techniques that more truthfully exhibit condominium preferences, without the hysteria from lease versus owner comparisons that sometimes portray heavier deductions on the leasing side.

First, it is wrong to compare the same proposed building from both a lease and an ownership viewpoint for tax and other analyses. What must be compared are the proposed building with *other* buildings in which leasing is available. In other words, the real choices should be faced.

More efficient use of space, fewer investment costs to start, more money-saving locations, and similar factors could mean a better cash flow position in condominium ownership in the particular building when sized against other alternatives in the same or nearby communities. In many instances, more consideration in original building construction may be given to an owner than would be the case with a lessee. Existing competitive rental space in the same locality may not exist at all, may be more than needed, or may be less than company requirements. Thus eventual lessee tax deductions may be offset by more costly business operations.

The businessman who prefers the ownership of his operating premises often has a better choice given by condominium than by leasing or full property ownership. It should be noted that although land cannot be depreciated by owners (whereas full rentals for use can be), the condominium owner buys only a percentage interest in land, thus not locking in a larger land cost that might pain if a fully owned site were sought. This factor of limited cost of land acquisition in a condominium, when added to others, might well make condominium operations more efficient.

Pooled use of expensive, or otherwise unavailable, equipment, and even staff, is another cost factor that could wipe out minor tax write-off comparisons.

Accelerated depreciation of buildings and equipment by condominium owners may in some cases provide larger cost deductions and faster return of investment cost than in the case of leasing.

Moreover, the importance of controlling one's own operation and preventing dilution of profits, key problems in many leasing arrangements, must be weighed against tax factors. In total perspective, differentials in tax treatment may be of limited significance. Current and future cash flow and freedom of operations are comparative factors that must be totaled in urging or rejecting the particulars of any one proposed condominium venture.

In summary, it is suggested that the business condominium requires a business cost analysis that includes income taxation as only one factor. Because of the utility of this new form of ownership, it is quite possible that operating and tax efficiencies in many cases would favor its selection over leasing. Never, however, should income tax factors alone be evaluated in a vacuum. Tax experts and business analysts are incompetent to advise on business condominium potential without the additional knowledge of the amazing flexibility and potential of this new form of business enterprise for achieving maximum profits and efficiencies from good planning.

CONCLUSIONS

The American history of real estate ownership has seen dramatic changes in ownership techniques occasioned by new requirements of business. Into this history now appears the business condominium, with characteristics that may in the future lead to widespread utilization of this new form.

As in the case of residential housing, the immense flexibility of the condominium format is the most remarkable characteristic of this form of ownership.

In reviewing the history of business real estate relationships, we have noted new techniques that arose from changing economic movements in American business. However, one can also cut through much of the new nomenclature to perceive lingering aspects of the feudal system that very much carry over into modern times. Under the feudal system, the tenant or serf paid over part of his crops to the landlord as a percentage tribute for the right to work the land. Subsequently quit rents were paid in place of payments in kind. The modern percentage lease arrangement may be far removed from the regulations of feudal tenure, but the concept of sharing production profits with landlords is very much alive, although the penalties are now limited to breach of contract rather than the harshness permitted in ancient times. Other remnants of the feudal system, such as the nature of crop to be planted and duties in connection therewith, also linger in modern agreements involving landlord and tenant.

The business condominium presents itself as a means for finally wiping out many of the heirlooms of the feudal system that have come down to us and been accepted in modern form as regular means for the conduct of business with respect to relationships steming from the nature of real estate ownership.

A revolution in real estate ownership, encouraged by use of the business condominium form, should inspire new freedom of operations and more initiative in American business.

CHAPTER IV

THE SALE-CONDOBACK

A NEW CONCEPT

The subject of this chapter is so new that it lacks a recognized name. We, therefore, descriptively call our subject the "sale-condoback." What we are talking about is an agreement whereby an owner of real property, usually improved, contracts to sell such property on condition that part of the same realty be deeded to him back in condominium unit form. Typically, with such device an owner can retain a valuable portion of real estate as an owner while cashing in on a substantial selling price for the rest of the property.

Many persons are more familiar with the term "sale-leaseback," which ordinarily involves complete divestiture of all title ownership by the seller, who then becomes a tenant or "lessee" of the new purchaser as part of simultaneous transactions.

We must evaluate the advantages and disadvantages of both methods to gauge adequately the potential of our new concept against the back-drop of more established real estate techniques. Once again, historical development of older methods must be explored to remove mere habit and automatic acceptance from the true needs and pressures of modern American industry.

THE SALE-LEASEBACK: SPLITTING INVESTMENT OWNERSHIP FROM OPERATIONS

The most usual purpose of a sale-leaseback for the business operator-owner is the liquidation of an investment position by change of ownership. It is an important current method of securing funds for capital expansion.

The sale-leaseback is most commonly thought of as the means for the total sale of property. In fewer instances, land or buildings physically severable, under ordinary conveyancing techniques, are divided for a partial leaseback transaction, with other portions of realty remaining in the same ownership. In many cases, however, the decision by an owner has to be "all or nothing" on selling his property because of legal or practical complexities that could ensue from partial sale of physically unseverable realty. Thus adjoining parking space might be sold off in a partial leaseback transaction by a large department store seeking to cash in on valuable investment property. But the fourth and fifth floors of a five-story building are another matter. As we have already noted, the complexities in the latter case can be solved by the business condominium.

Thousands of sales transactions each year are keyed to leases retained by sellers for partial space. The candy store owner who sells a five-story building that also houses his store may not call his transaction by the formidable sale-leaseback nomenclature, even though he enters a 5-year lease as part of the transaction.

Beginning in the latter part of the nineteenth century, the breakup of resident industry also resulted in many investor purchases of residential buildings with one or more stores on street level.

Probably the first substantial use of sale-leasebacks by institutions in the United States was to shield property owners from the stigma of running sweatshops in New York City around the start of World War I. Buildings were bought by investors and then leased back to the institutions on a total, carefree lease arrangement whereby insurance companies and other institutions were given full building control as lessees, together with the burdens of dealing with businesses engaging in sweatshop activities. As in almost every case until the end of World War II, these sale-leasebacks covered an entire building and parcel, even though the buildings were multitenanted structures.

Because of state limitations on investments of insurance companies, the great sale-leaseback boom after World War II was germinated by transactions aimed at circumventing the laws. True, some grocery supermarket chains had used the sale-leaseback in the late 1930s, but with little national significance. It was the insurance industry that brought the method into formidable use.

Until the middle of the 1940–1950 decade, state laws generally barred the acquisition of nonresidential properties by insurance companies. Nevertheless, some insurance companies managed to make, in effect, almost 100 percent "loans" to alleged purchasers who were not much more than dummy title holders for the lenders. In those years tax-exempt colleges were in an enviable tax position to accept a small annual income for services as purchaser. The operating lessee would contract a direct set of obligations to the insurance company "lender" and thereby place the insurance company in a position tantamount to a purchaser-lessor in just about every way but name.

The interest by insurance companies in the sale-leaseback technique had been stirred considerably in 1943 by the well-publicized sale by Gimbels of its huge Philadelphia department store to a tax-exempt trust formed to benefit several universities, with Gimbels leasing back the store after its sale. Top insurance companies immediately put their legal departments to work to evolve strategies for taking advantage of this new technique in financial investment. Most attractive were the features of heavy loans to high-credit businesses together with the increasingly popular arrangement of having tenants pay a rent "net" of all operating and maintenance expenditures, thus leaving the lease "carefree" for the lessor seeking passive investments.

Pressure by insurance companies to propose changes in state restrictions against owning nonresidential realty came from two chief causes. In the early 1940s, industrial and public utility corporations refunded numerous debt obligations, widely held by insurance companies, to take advantage of declining interest rates. This left considerable funds for immediate investment. Then, after the conclusion of World War II, demand by industry for new funds and expansion moved to historic highs.

Virginia, in 1942, began the trend to permit nonresidential real estate purchases by insurance companies, although it was limited to a percentage of company assets. From 1945 through 1947 a large number of states followed with similarly liberal enabling legislation. The sale-leaseback by long-term net lease became the commonplace and convenient implementation of this new authority. By the net lease, the seller-tenant took on most burdens of operating costs and maintenance. In later years, mainly when noninstitutional fee owners were involved, the tenants in leaseback transactions even paid the owner's fee mortgage obligation directly to the mortgagee, in what was sometimes called a "net-net lease."

In their search for secure investments, the insurance industry often underestimated the future appreciation value of the real estate targeted for sale-leaseback transactions. Their analysts were concerned principally with lending money, often adding leasehold mortgages to purchase fund allocations, in order to achieve maximum investment. Such mortgaging renewed the leasehold as security for loans and restored to popularity, but with more cautious terms, a financing device which as we noted had fallen into disfavor in the 1930s. Thus an insurance company would purchase the fee interest of a property for 6 million dollars, and also give a 3 million dollar mortgage on the leasehold to the seller-tenant, thereby investing 150 percent of the property's appraised value. Mostly, emphasis was on the *credit lease* to highly rated businesses rather than on investment risk for capital appreciation opportunities. It was believed that a 100 percent (and higher) investment had to be practically riskless, and that the key security was the credit standing of the tenant over the long term involved.

Although some provision for increased rentals was made, often by periodic land reappraisal formulas, for the most part the insurance companies purchasing did not foresee the tremendous future demand for well-situated commercial and industrial realty. Otherwise they would not have tied their hands on income potential. This error was one frustrating factor causing institutional lenders to seek equity "kickers" in later years, rather than merely settling for the original type of sale-leaseback return calculated at a single moment but for a duration of many years. Attractiveness to realty owners was continually diminished as more and more demands for equity and income participation were demanded in sale-leaseback propositions.

What was good enough for insurance companies now attracted other institutional and private investors as well. High-credit-rated companies well-heeled with real estate, such as chains like Sears, Roebuck and Company, found it relatively easy to sell groups of stores, offices, or outlets to major insurance companies and other investors. Tremendous legal and accounting effort went into formulation of sale-leaseback documentation; a new area of expertise was born for brokers, managers, appraisers, and others.

In the late 1950s hundreds of limited partnership investment syndicates were formed in the United States for the purpose of entering sale-leaseback transactions. Unlike the initial use of the form for high-credit tenants, the form was also employed for rankly speculative deals covering bowling alleys, ski areas, motels, and a multitude of risky businesses. More stable syndicates sought multitenanted office and loft buildings or established factories and warehouses. Common to all these arrangements were profit-squeezing rental participation agreements. This latter factor, plus a constant turnover of properties at higher sales prices, led to the collapse of many syndicates in the early 1960s. Nevertheless, for sound and practical reasons we have indicated, the sale-leaseback was continued as an established method of real estate investment.

Owners confronted in the past 20 years with the need for more cash had a new method available besides borrowing by way of an original or refinanced mortgage. To many, the sale-leaseback appeared attractive because they could thereby obtain a huge selling price for an entire property, still retaining effective operations on the premises protected by a long-term leasing arrangement.

The same pressures and difficulties surrounding long-term leases obviously accompany the sale-leaseback, if not more so. Today, a purchaser expending huge outlays seeks every possible form of profit sharing and inflationary safeguard. Can a method be found that would eliminate some of these intrusions on the businessman seeking to sell his property but to retain operating control? The business condominium may be one important way.

The business condominium has not yet become a formidable competitor to the sale-leaseback. The former was almost unknown until the early 1960s, and will have to await disenchantment with leasing arrangements, which are to a large extent profit-sharing contracts. Those who propose consideration of the business condominium as an alternative to the sale-leaseback must encourage real estate professionals to turn away from basic assumptions and meticulously prepared sale-leaseback documentation, which after 20 years of experience and education are widely understood.

OVERCOMING LEASEBACK DISADVANTAGES WITH CONDOBACKS

There will be times when sale-leaseback techniques will prove quite adequate to the business operating entrepreneur. On the other hand, he has thus far been quite limited in his alternatives. He usually reviewed three other possibilities: remaining in his present role of property owner, seeking new or additional mortgage financing, or remaining as owner of the realty which he might rent to another firm after removal of his own business operations from the premises. Ownership, however, had to be completely retained or completely abandoned.

Introduction of the condoback method now presents another major alternative for appropriate cases, especially those in which only partial space is required by the present owner. Here ownership can be partially retained and partially abandoned.

Before specifically reviewing the advantages of condobacks, it might do well to reflect on general analytic factors applicable to the other methods that confront the decision maker.

He must consider the present and future cost of money borrowed from banks or others. Oftentimes, key terms of mortgages are conditioned by the amount of the mortgage needed, with larger requirements bringing more onerous clauses on interest, prepayment, loan duration, and so on.

The owner must ponder his income tax liability if he sells his property or later receives rental income. In that connection, the use and availability of depreciation methods and other fast write-offs of costs are pertinent.

The value of his property to others now and in the future is another point for thought. This is based not only on the value of his business operation, but also on other uses of present buildings and even raw land.

Another subject, distinct from real estate technique analysis, is the availability of new equity investments from new associates, or even "going public" for infusion of public funds by the sale of securities or the liquidation of part of the owner's equity by public sale of stock. This method involves a dilution of full ownership.

In discussing some of the disadvantages of sale-leasebacks, we also implicitly cover some disadvantages in other methods, while pointing out some distinct advantages of the condoback technique. But full analysis of all methods would be essential in every case being considered. Importantly, however, the sale-condoback looms as a new and vital subject in such discussion.

LEASES TEND TO FAVOR LANDLORDS

By using the condominium approach in a condoback arrangement, the tons of boiler plate lease clauses favoring landlords are avoided. As a general proposition, leases tend to favor landlords in many important ways. When a sale-leaseback is created, the tremendous immediate investment of cash by the purchaser-lessor is usually accompanied by more stringent tenant burdens than usual. So concerned, and rightfully so, is the purchaser about defeasance of the valuable credit lease, that he can be expected to obtain contractual concessions cementing the lessee into long-term specific conduct and obligations that remove substantial freedom of operations.

CONDOBACKS CAN MEAN SMALLER MORTGAGE OBLIGATIONS

The result of a sale-leaseback to the seller is a position of tenancy. Whereas *leasehold* mortgages may be available to him should he wish additional cash for whatever reason, they tend to contain higher interest terms as well as demanding requirements for landlord waiver of many ordinary rights of title in favor of leasehold security. Often, leasehold mortgages are smaller percentages of security value than fee types; in other words, the amount of cash based on the leasehold security tends to be smaller than for fee title security. The condoback seller takes back the fee title and good mortgageable security under most state laws. Because of the superiority of fee title security over that of leaseholds, financial institutions are likely to provide more liberal terms for mortgages. Moreover, one can expect greater freedom in the condominium owner to recast, refinance, and extend mortgages than that available to lessees for leasehold mortgages. A leasehold mortgage will rarely be backed up by a second or third leasehold mortgage on the same security. On the other hand, second mortgages on fee title of good commercial property are not unusual at all.

It should also be noted that the use of a condoback can achieve a cutback of existing mortgage obligation because of the smaller financing required on the reduced space. This provides good balance sheet results, without having to assume the role of tenant.

CONDOBACKS PROVIDE FLEXIBILITY FOR SALE OF PROPERTY

An owner of property pondering a condoback of partial space has considerable flexibility for future planning not available to the all-or-nothing leaseback seller. The condoback seller has any of the following advantages:

1. He can rid himself of all space he does not actually now use.

2. He can retain for his own use all space now needed plus additional reserve space for future expansion.

3. He can retain more condominium units than his operations require, renting them temporarily on short-term leases. This may be done to obtain income temporarily for space unneeded presently but necessary later for company expansion. Or he may wish to hold for rental some additional units, then later sell various segments of his property in years

when values are high or when his tax position will be most favorable, as when ordinary income is low and the effect of depreciation recapture lessened.

4. He can obtain only those new funds actually needed. He may not have an immediate business use for the large selling price resulting from a complete sale, as would flow from the sale-leaseback. Funds for which he is pressed might be available from a condoback transaction in an amount equal to current needs.

5. Instead of adding to an existing fee mortgage on the total property, the condoback results in a smaller mortgage for the owner, the obtaining of additional funds by sale of remaining space, and the avoidance of the loss of valuable property. Some sale-leasebacks have been entered when owners were unable to obtain additional mortgage financing because borrowings were already too large for the security value of the total property, resulting in the loss of ownership through forced leasebacks. The condoback should now be considered as an alternative when this sort of financing bind comes about. Even if a tight money market is current, condominium flexibility may sometimes extricate an owner from a seemingly impossible money situation.

GREATER MOBILITY

Because the value of the leaseback arrangement to the purchaser is founded on long-term credit dependency, the likelihood of permission for the seller's easy removal from premises is customarily slight indeed. Even if subleasing or economic abandonment is allowed, it is often at the price of continued rent obligation or severe penalties. This loss of essential business freedom to relocate can painfully hamper business efficiency in later periods. Commercial reversals may require prompt termination of total or partial business operations. Rentals may prove excessively harsh during periods of recession. Opportunities for more attractive space utilization might have to be bypassed, or business segments might have to be separated inefficiently when more extensive quarters are required either for the same operation or for combination with other techniques necessary in company planning.

The condoback unit owner will ordinarily gain much more mobility than the long-term tenant on a leaseback. The former may offer for sale his fee title, and its successful consummation means prompt removal for whatever reasons. The difference between full ownership and lease-backing is pointed out somewhat by a recent typical business calamity. Large corporations that guaranteed leasebacks by hamburger and similar franchise owners have sometimes suffered enormous losses before extricating themselves from a host of poor earning situations. The land-building owners had purchased and leased back largely on the basis of the food concerns' outstanding credit. But the failure of many franchises to earn minimum rental expenses left the guaranteeing companies in the untenable position of settling further lease obligations by costly forfeiture or other drastic financial settlements.

CONDOBACKS OFFER OPPORTUNITIES FOR APPRECIATION

An operating business firm investing in the real estate that houses its activities often considers three possible avenues for profit.

1. Income from regular business activities.
2. The eventual profit on sale or exchange of realty.
3. The immediate cash flow from mortgage refinancing.

Some of America's major railroads, as well as those of our neighbors, probably could not have continued to service the public for the past 40 years without substantial profits emanating from partial sales of realty (including airspace) in the vicinity of, or over, the rail lines. Many a business firm has been bailed out of operating troubles by a lucrative sell-off of its commercial realty. With land and rental costs as high as they have risen, imaginative thought must be given the selection of business sites. One of the areas for analysis is the potential for realty appreciation. Sometimes value increases enormously merely by the entry into the area of a prestige company. It is well known that better companies attract their like when striking into untested areas.

When a leasehold exists and land and buildings have appreciated in value, pressures increase for landlord participation in the increase through higher rentals. Each uncontemplated eventuality needing landlord approval tends to become a discussion largely centered on increased rentals. Ownership by condominium permits the unit owner's fee title interest to appreciate in value mainly for his exclusive betterment. Although leases sometimes can be assigned (assuming landlord permission), often the price of landlord approval to a mere tenant is a sharing in selling-price profits and higher rentals for the lease purchaser. The latter factor reduces the original lessee's potential for profit. As the condominium unit owner's reality increases in value, the mortgaging potential becomes larger. However, when leasehold mortgages are sources of additional revenue to leaseback tenants, permission may be required of the landlord who will, at the same time, seek to add rental increases, including profit-sharing factors. So to speak, the lessor may get a "second shot" to review profit-sharing clauses based on the actual performance of his tenant.

Condominium appreciation possibilities, however, must be reviewed against arguments that purchasing ties up otherwise useable cash. Availability of substantial mortgage funds can, however, reduce the use of cash by purchasers, so that net cash requirements are usually much lower than a total purchase price. Leasing brokers often slur over the latter point when trying to create sale-leaseback transactions.

APPROVAL OF NEW PARTICIPANTS ON RESALES

The landlord-tenant axis in the sale-leaseback is regularly shaken by sale or assignment of the lessor's ownership. Different attitudes may be infused by outright sale of fee title, subject to the long-term lease originated as a sale-leaseback. Also prevalent are "sandwich" concoctions by which the prime lessor assigns total lessee net rentals to another party for a lump-sum payment and smaller rentals over a specific period of time. This type of outcome can be expected when percentage rentals turn into lucrative profit-sharing transactions. Such freedom by the owner to sell or subdivide his ownership results in new, unforeseen participants in the lessee's rental relationships. The higher the price paid for full title or intermediary position by a newcomer, the more unreasonable his attitude may be on matters requiring landlord approval or renegotiation. Customarily, lessees in sale-leasebacks must obtain landlord approval to assign away their position and obligations. Just as customarily, the lessor has no similar obligation to the lessee.

On the other hand, the condoback purchaser does not have similar worries of changing control and speculation applicable to his operating premises owned by condominium deed. Nevertheless, grouping does mean that approvals by a condominium government require amity among unit owners. But the approval problem in most cases centers on seeking the *common* good in managing common areas, and not continually squeezing profits from activities of other participants. The *right of first refusal* sometimes found in condominium bylaws can safeguard against entry into the condominium community by financially unstable companies. By this right, the elected board of managers can match the best purchase offer made for another owner's unit. However, some recent cases of restrictive rental clauses in shopping centers (not involving condominiums) raise doubts as to whether refusal of new entrants can be motivated by refusal to admit new competition from similar businesses.

Just as the proximity of other firms needed for more efficient operation (suppliers of raw materials, for example) is an attractive feature when, initially considering a condominium venture on its formation, this factor no doubt will play a role in decision making on the right of first refusal on resales.

RENTAL VERSUS OWNER TAX COSTS

In addition to reviewing the other comparative factors discussed in this chapter as well as the specific requirements of a company for space, some mathematics are helpful, although they are certainly not definitive when standing alone.

Assuming two possibilities only, one for total leaseback, the other for a condoback of partial space, the following annual income tax analysis can be of aid.

FOR THE LEASEBACK TENANT: Income (net of all but rental expenses) less annual rental expense equals income on which tax is payable.

FOR THE CONDOBACK OWNER: Income (net of all but depreciation allowance and without mortgage amortization subtraction) less annual depreciation allowance equals income on which tax is payable.

Merely to give arbitrary figures for these formulas would be misleading. Lease terms and purchase prices are too varying to be placed in standardized patterns. Unfortunately, most leasing brokers are adept at playing this game to achieve apparently glowing results for their own purposes. Once these professionals comprehend the tremendous brokerage commissions also possible from condobacks, their optimism may shift or at least be shared.

In some situations either the leaseback or condoback will look clearly preferable at first, especially from a tax viewpoint. But really thorough analysis must cut through established custom and highlight benefits to business not immediately measureable by the kind of simple income tax formula given above (for example, the incidence of landlord participation in future profits that may dramatically increase rentals in later periods).

TAX STRATEGY FOR THE CONDOBACK PURCHASER: THE BUILDING OWNER

The income tax consequences of the condoback will constitute an important concern to all parties to the transaction. For purposes of clarity, we view the positions of building owner and lessee separately when each considers a condoback. The building owner will form a condominium and take back one or more units while selling off the rest of his property. In the second kind of condoback, the present tenant will buy the entire building, convert it to condominium status and take back one or more units for his own use. The latter could be operating as tenant of partial space or under a total building lease. In the latter instance the current tenant plans to buy the entire building but condoback to himself only part of the space.

Let us look first at the position of a building owner who wishes to convert to condominium with a condoback result. In some instances, the owner will be fully or partially tax-exempt because of the religious or charitable nature of the activity performed on premises. Nonprofit medical insurance societies and some religious groups have already negotiated condobacks recently. To the extent that there is tax exemption on the sales of premises, there is that much less worry about our problem of income taxes. On the other hand, the ordinary business firm owning the building does have distinct tax considerations, some of which will become clearer as the Treasury Department faces the questions presented by condobacks. We shall try to identify these questions, and hopefully attempt to offer some help. But the reader is cautioned that his own highly competent tax counsel is essential in each individual case in this new and complex area of tax law.

As with most realty decision making, tax analysis most often centers on maximizing the availability of cash. The owner of a building considering a condoback of partial space may have already used most of the owner depreciation allowances permitted by the Internal Revenue Code. The catch-up of amortization payments, which are not deductible items (as against remaining depreciation) might result in income tax being paid on monies not retained before taxes. The owner confronted with an immediate need for cash for his own business enterprise on the premises or elsewhere could explore whether a condoback vehicle would be more lucrative than applying for mortgage funds from institutional or private lenders; this is especially important if the building has already been mortgaged to its maximum potential. At a particular moment, an offer from tenants might be exceedingly productive of good cash results, and an excellent source of needed funds. Other interesting possibilities for condobacks exist when normal operations of the building consistently have been at a loss, or recently have become so expensive and burdensome as not to be worthwhile for continuation of full ownership. In these latter cases the condoback may be an alternative to forced selling, even forestalling bankruptcy in some cases.

It should be pointed out that many varieties of real estate arrangements can be employed with the flexible condoback device. For example, an owner may wish to enlarge substantially or to rehabilitate his premises. The funds available from purchasers of condominium units can help greatly without additional debt obligations incurred by the owner of the building. Thus it might even be practical in some instances by the condoback method for the owner of a building to retain in total his original building space, which originally was not physically shareable with others, by adding additional stories or extending portions of the building for use of new condominium entrants.

By the sale of a portion of his building as business condominium units, the owner faces Internal Revenue Code Sections 1231 and 1250 with capital gains type tax burdens for the real property (with Section 1245 obligations for personal property included in the sale). The impact of the recapture of depreciation will be felt when profits are obtained by the seller, computed in direct relation to his current tax basis. However, a most important feature of the condoback should be realized. *Because the sale is partial, the owner may be able to shelter profit otherwise taxable if the entire building had been sold.* In effect, careful planning can result in a partial sale that liquidates inherent building appreciated value without the full burden of taxation, including recapture of depreciation. Perhaps, this form of method will be added as a regular business concept to the currently popular installment sale of property, by which the owner gives up his title and space; and added to such curiosities as the sale-buy back which is, in effect, a contractual arrangement for obtaining sale proceeds and the right to reinstate ownership on an installment basis by repurchase. It would appear that the sale of condobacks would be less plagued with tax dangers than some of the other techniques that have developed in recent years. In effect, the condoback simply is a bona fide sale of part of the property to others. It is done without the seller giving up fee ownership to certain space and without the necessity for installment or buy-back arrangements that fuse various sections of the Internal Revenue Code.

Competent tax counsel is required to avoid the chief danger that might result in a condoback transaction. This would be the characterization of the sale of condominium units as the work of a *dealer* rather than an investor, with the onerous result that total profit on the sale would be taxable as ordinary income. However, it is hoped that the Internal Revenue will not take such a view inconsistent with what is really happening, the bona fide partial sale of one's long-owned investment property. Moreover, the transaction should be arranged as far as possible so that all, or at least most, negotiations for the sale of units in the new condominium regime would be completed before any transfer of title takes place to unit purchasers, to avoid the original owner having in his hands any unsold units after he begins unit transfers to others. The utilization of intermediary sponsors to take by sale the entire remaining space for resale could help avoid the original owner's being charged with trading with an inventory; but to the extent such arrangement is not at arms length there are serious tax questions possible. Use of the installment sale or other income-spreading devices permitted by the Internal Revenue Code can minimize tax burdens even if ordinary income rates must be applied.

It would seem that the mere division into a condominium of a single existing property and its bona fide sale on a condoback basis, even if some units must be marketed over a substantial period of time, should not be accorded ordinary income tax treatment if the delay results from poor reception of the offering. Perhaps, if the popularity of this form becomes extensive, a new provision of the revenue law should be enacted to clarify tax results.

If the condominium is created for prompt sale by an investor of his long-held existing property, it is merely a convenient selling device for partial sale of his property. If it is created to convert an investment building into a continual marketplace for sale of units and their trading and resale, the danger of dealer status will lurk in each transaction. However, if a builder constructs a new commercial condominium or a large number of new units with condoback to himself and the marketing of the new units, he would probably be classified as a dealer for the new units, much the same as the builder of a group of one-family homes who retains one for his own residence or for rental investment. Whether an owner should be treated as a dealer for converting existing units in a hybrid offering also involving newly added units remains as an interesting question.

Whatever the characterization, dealer or investor, given the taxpayer taking the condoback, there is less likelihood that he will convince authorities that disposition proceeds from remaining units should not all be accorded the same tax treatment. There have been instances in which the same owner of noncondominium, unrelated properties was judged a dealer in one case and an investor in others, based on variance in the ostensible purposes of his physically separate holdings. Perhaps this distinguishing attitude might be available among condominium units in the same regime, although the proximity of units may prove a stumbling block to clear thinking. For example, let us assume that in a condoback transaction involving entirely new construction, the developer takes back two of four unsold units to hold for his own company operations in later years. Query whether the latter units should place the taxpayer in the same classification, upon sale in later years, as the two other units admitted to have been retained for prompt resale?

Now we'll turn to another question. As far as the right to depreciate is concerned, it would seem that the condoback owner retains his same basis as allocated to property comprising and remaining in his condoback unit, and would continue to take depreciation deductions accordingly. A mathematical exertion is necessary to ferret the residue basis from the new interest in common elements. A first owner in a new construction condoback condominium would, of course, commence a program that can utilize the maximum accelerated depreciation allowable. Care should be taken to assure that interim relationships do not collapse first-owner status.

In any form of condoback, careful analysis and expert advice are necessary in allocating purchase prices between land and improvements. The owner of an existing building, for example, may want the highest cost possible to be placed on the land, to reduce depreciation recapture. The purchaser, on the other hand, might want the opposite result to establish the highest possible tax basis for depreciation, because land is not a depreciable item for cost write-offs on tax returns. In the condominium condoback transaction, the analyst must move an additional step from breakdown of land and improvement cost.

Assuming land to be a common element, the formula to be followed probably would be in most cases:

Total value assigned to total condominium land divided by condoback owner's percentage in the common elements. The resulting amount is then subtracted from total land value. This gives ordinarily the land selling price for remaining units.

The common interest also will be an eventual factor in determining land pricing on an eventual sale of an individual unit, when tax factors will make a land–sales-price allocation important.

TAX STRATEGY FOR THE CONDOBACK: THE TENANT BUYER

Many a tenant leasing partial space in existing business buildings in the future will reflect on the practicality and profitableness of seeking to buy the entire building with a condoback of partial space.

The purchase of the building itself ordinarily is not a taxable event for the buyer, but the resale to other tenants or outsiders by the condoback purchaser is a taxable transaction to the extent of computed differential between the allocated purchase and selling prices. In view of the fact that part of the purchased property is taken back as a condominium unit, it probably will be urged that the transaction be viewed realistically as the purchase of a total building and a resale of all but reserved space. It would seem unjustified by reality to look at the transactions as the purchase and resale of separate units, irrespective that the condominium is formed after purchase of the entire building. If logic governs here, the lessee-purchaser can shelter the unit prices he receives by nearly all building cost. This result is urgently important because the entire profit on such condoback arrangement will likely fall into ordinary income, especially if it is swiftly consummated. If, on the other hand, the building is purchased by a tenant and held for a considerable time before conversion to condominium, the possibility arises of Section 1231 investment treatment. We may expect arguments in the latter instance that the tenant's continued presence after the sale of units demonstrates a continuous intent from the beginning for long-term operation of the building.

Once the tenant is a condominium owner, his depreciation picture may change. Unamortized improvements made by him as lessee would continue to be written off on the remaining basis, but now by way of depreciation, because unlimited fee ownership necessarily exceeds the life of any improvement. If the lessee had already partially depreciated an improvement, usually because its life was shorter than the lease term, such depreciation allowance on his tax return would probably be continued without change. In addition, the condoback unit cost, less the share paid for the undivided interest in land, should be depreciable ordinarily under the same rules applicable to other purchases of fee interests in commercial property, including the available accelerated methods.

Whereas a tenant's portion of rent used by his landlord to pay mortgage amortization is still deductible by the tenant, such deduction is no longer allowed when the tenant shifts to condominium owner. Mortgage amortization will no longer be a deductible item. However, the tenant has received a loan of mortgage proceeds which he is repaying, his purchase enabling him to take advantage of property appreciation and other owner benefits. The latter factors did not exist for the tenant.

BUSINESS STRATEGY FOR THE CONDOBACK: THE TENANT BUYER

Most discussions the author has heard on the business condominium centered on carrying charge differentials between ownership and tenancy. Certainly a cost analysis should be attempted in each case to determine as far as possible what changes would result from condominium. In the tenant-condoback situation, comparisons have much more relevancy than usual because it is the very same space, in the very same building, that is the subject for study.

The purchase prices paid by others for units may provide *front money* for financing the purchase of your own unit at little or no cost.

A lease may soon terminate and the outlook be uncertain. Even if the condominium carrying charges are higher than present rentals, they may be lower than renegotiated rentals on the new lease.

Profit-sharing clauses automatically in effect may soon raise rentals considerably above condominium carrying charges.

An urgent need for new space right now requires an immediate decision to move, unless additional space can be found on the same premises. By condoback the latter might be facilitated.

Company requirements for future operations necessitate early planning for reserves of future space near or contiguous to present operations. A condoback coupled with ownership of other units temporarily rented may provide the answer.

A good commercial mortgage market can ease marketability of other units at good prices. To delay may make the venture difficult later, as well as preventing permanent capture of your premises by fee ownership.

Sale of the total building by the owner to another investor may bring a new landlord with oppressive rental ideas, or one who may decide not to renew your lease. Purchase by your firm would be too large and unneeded an undertaking. The condoback would bring relief from a shift of ownership and permit purchase of premises without tying up the greater funds necessary to purchase an entire building.

Ownership by condoback can give a guaranty of prestigious decoration and location well beyond the capability of mere tenancy. In the interim period of full ownership, the eventual condoback owner can provide in bylaws for the renaming of the building and for outside decorative markings that would be most helpful for business advertising, prestige, and operations.

It is quite possible that the total value of some buildings will be upped considerably after their division into condominium units, as against the price available from single purchasers who would act as ordinary lessors.

OUTSIDE BUYERS AND CONDOBACKS

We should not forget that outsiders, nonowners and nontenants, may also consider the purchase of commercial buildings with condobacks of certain units to themselves. The combination of front money from unit purchasers and good bank financing for the total purchase and resale of separate units might together create a financial picture that is quite attractive. The result would be company space owned in fee simple, acquired with considerable help by the funds of others.

Passive investors may consider engaging in the same kind of transaction, although the end result would be renting the condoback acquired at the conclusion of the negotiations.

CONTENTS OF CONDOBACK CONTRACTS

Initial condoback agreements will not all be alike, because of different contracting parties possible. For example, an agreement may cover a current owner of property who is contracting with a group of his tenants. Or, the agreement could be initiated by a tenant wishing to purchase the piece of property to convert the structure to condominium in which he will own one or more units by subsequent filing of the declaration and issuance of condominium deeds to other participants for the remainder of the property. Contracts between a current resident owner and a group of tenants would ordinarily provide that the owner agrees to file a declaration converting a rental structure to a condominium, with units created for each of the participants, including the current owner of the building who will take back partial space in condominium form.

In any case, such agreements should provide for the eventual filing of a declaration of condominium and bylaws by the owner or other sponsors with the appropriate government authority as required by the particular jurisdiction that is the situs for the building. Preferably, such documents should be attached to the agreement and made a part thereof, to assure that the rights of all parties are clearly defined at this early stage. Signed memoranda of understanding containing vague phraseology would seem good candidates for later problems.

To get to the point of actual contract it will have been necessary for all parties to negotiate at length. Such items as space allocations, responsibilities for maintenance charges, and voting power are not matters better left for later occasions past contract time. It is possible to contract merely on the basis of minimum generalities, or to go a step further and outline the basic contents of documents to be prepared later. However, for purposes of protecting the rights of all parties, it is highly desirable that no contract be signed by any of the parties unless the specific future form of declaration and bylaws are affixed to the agreement.

If a tenant purchases a building from a nonresident owner for purposes of conversion to condominium, the initial contract of sale would merely contain ordinary language for the purchase of an existing property from an owner who is to leave the scene. On the other hand, if the current owner of the building wishes to retain rental space therein later, he would have to be assured the future condominium declaration would be subject to such proviso. *In effect, a sale-leaseback and sale-condoback would be combined.*

Unlike most arrangements for the purchase of buildings which can use simple form contracts merely denoting the legal description of property and emphasizing good title availability, the contract among participants for condominium would require much more detail. Sometimes such agreement is the first in line of arrangement, as when an owner contracts with tenants for condominium, with the owner taking back a unit. More often, such an agreement follows in sequence the contract for simple purchase of the property, as when a tenant buys property for condoback. However, it may occasionally be possible to condition the outright purchase of property on the success in obtaining a condominium agreement with other tenants or outsiders by a date certain. Once a binding agreement to purchase the premises is entered, problems that pose obstructions to consummating the entire transaction could leave the purchaser hanging in the air with a building that cannot be converted to condominium.

Especially if the participant contract does not have the proposed declaration annexed, future unit owners are bound to seek protective clauses in their initial contract among themselves. In the course of negotiation one can expect reference to such matters as access to front, side, and back entrances and roadways; use of loading platforms; availability of storage space; advertising signs; parking facilities; management selection and obligations; voting rights; the uses to be made of other units; the method of computation of maintenance charge payments, especially as related to any current rental differences among current tenants; budgeting; air conditioning hours; metering by utilities; the protective security system; and insurance methods.

More complexity in contracting may be expected if new construction of any substantial amount is to be undertaken as part of the promotional venture. If large areas of space are not yet taken, and if a major space occupant must still be found, some leeway must be given for changes in final plans to suit newcomers. Nevertheless, the initial contracts should protect against unreasonable constriction or extension of space requirements of other unit owners, horizontally, vertically, and curvaceously, to avoid radically altering contemplated units.

CHAPTER V

MANAGEMENT OF BUSINESS CONDOMINIUMS

THE STAGES OF RESPONSIBILITY

The function of management for the commercial condominium is performed most usually at two levels, by the elected board of managers and by the managing agent appointed to carry out the policies of the board. Because we are dealing with business ventures, as distinguished from residential housing, many firms may also possess an internal management division which acts in liaison with the central condominium administration. In this chapter we shall endeavor to discern the responsibilities of each group as they face the relatively new and unique condominium form of ownership of commercial quarters.

When divergent business interests are coupled with commonly used areas, one might well expect conflict and problems, in the absence of intelligent and sensitive coordination of exclusive with common interests. To a considerable degree, management personnel on all levels must thoroughly comprehend the methodology, benefits and limitations of the condominium technique to maximize economic and social advantages in its use.

THE THREE PRINCIPLES OF CONDOMINIUM MANAGEMENT

Our analysis of techniques and detail at all stages of management focuses on the three underlying factors making for good or bad management.

1. Assuring exclusiveness to each unit owner.
2. Assuring harmonious use of commonly used facilities.
3. Protecting common areas restricted to fewer than all unit owners.

MENTAL ATTITUDE FOR GOVERNMENT

The key psychological undertow inhibiting efficient board operations will no doubt be an overt disinterest in the affairs of other participants. This varies with the building's specialty use and its prestige for attracting customers and clients.

Serving on the board of managers ordinarily results in more concern for the common good if the building has a specialty, for instance, a professional building housing medical practitioners. This same concern appears in specialty warehouse condominiums and scientific research developments. The reason may be the similarity of interest among participants. In addition, an expensive prestige location adds desire for effective group action, to assure maintenance of building stature.

More problems in board member attitude can be expected in buildings in which condominium units are owned by relatively unrelated business firms, as would be the case for a combination restaurant-warehouse-offices condominium. Although interest there may be, in the latter type of situation, in one's own operations the ability to sympathize with special problems of other unit owners would tend to be more limited. By-laws and declarations in the latter case need to be more specific and foreseeing, leaving as little as possible to the whims of a possibly disinterested board.

THE DECISION FOR BOARD REPRESENTATION

Before any discussion is possible on the organization of condominium government, exemplified by a board of managers or directors, we must answer one query to which our discussion has led. Should the board of managers be a small group representing the entire membership? Or, should each business firm have its own representative on the board?

In condominiums containing just a few participants, we have found the almost universal practice of having all unit owners on the board, often with equally weighted voting rights. When a large number of unit members are involved, the problem often is not simple to solve, the problem really being fear of overreaching by others where representation is lacking.

In residential condominiums, representation by a small, elected group is practiced more regularly because most unit owners have similar problems with respect to amenities and services. The commercial owners in a business condominium, however, may be conducting occupations radically different in scope in the use of facilities and demand for services. Representation by others may sometimes not be reliable if the interests of unit owners are sharply different. One method for handling this problem is to require entire membership approval for certain key management decisions.

From the very outset of planning the development of a business condominium, careful consideration must be given to the problem of eventual internal government. If uncaring, lackadaisical attention is paid this subject, many otherwise interested prospective purchasers may turn away because of fear of the lack of business control.

MANAGEMENT DOCUMENTS WRITTEN TO DATE

Examination by the author of a substantial number of condominium documents for business ventures in various parts of the world leads to the conclusion that many such agreements have been inadequately drafted and only sparsely relate to many of the important factors of the condominium relationship that should be covered. For example, in Puerto Rico and South America the use of detailed bylaws and governing rules for operation often just does not exist, with only vague generalities contained in governing documents. It would appear in many cases that a more general framework of language is used compared with the more specific detail found in residential documentation in the respective countries. Several European and South American countries, such as France and Brazil, have continually enacted new legislation with more comprehensive coverage of a host of areas, thus excusing more elaborate documentation on some major points.

In the United States, commercial condominium documentation either wallows in considerable vagueness in many instances, or has been impaired, often by the mere copying of the language used in residential condominium documents. Thus there is substantial need to study the composite factors important to the business condominium that should result in bylaws and other documentation that are custom tailored to the particular business ventures involved. The tendency in the United States merely to repeat as boiler plate many of the clauses in residential condominiums should be replaced by a more thorough evaluation of the special problems of the business ventures.

With the above perspective, we shall attempt to point to special problems that may exist in business condominiums that should be in some way covered by the underlying documentation found in declarations, bylaws, and so on. Not all condominium ventures will or should cover all relationships in the same way; some should treat certain problems inordinately, in accordance with the uniqueness of the regime.

THE SELECTION PROCESS

In the final analysis, management in the commercial condominium resides within the framework of unit owner power. True, each unit owner has voting rights and, especially in larger groupings, must to a considerable extent rely on appointed officers and employees for much of the policy and detail of daily management decisions. Yet the results that lead to compatibility and smoothness in the venture to a large degree stem from the initial process of selection wherefrom came the unit owners themselves. Most business condominium developments in the United States have been presold before the filing of master documents that finalized formation of the condominium. The participants could, therefore, have been brought together in direct confrontation prior to creation of the new business format by which they would be joined.

In many business ventures of this type, the preselection process is the key to eventual success. In Europe and South America, many commercial condominiums were first syndicated by the future owners primarily with their own venture capital, thereby leading to the determination of the identities of future participants while in the informal, noncontractual stage, except for investors craving anonymity who used agents as covers. In the United States, preselection has often occurred without planning for this important feature. Most business condominiums here have involved new construction or substantial rehabilitation or reconstruction before the consummation of the joint venture. Even though outside developers and institutional lenders financed the construction stage, the practicalities of financing led to requirements, especially by banks, for preselling of a major portion of total units. In addition, without knowing the identity of unit owners, it would have been extremely difficult to create satisfactorily spaced units for future commercial and industrial tenants. During the selling phases, many purchasers cautiously conditioned their participation on their clearance of other proposed participants. There has probably been less cloaking of investor identification than in any other area of commercial real estate investment.

A variety of business specialties may sometimes be essential in promoting the venture. It is probable, for example, that a dermatologist considering a medical condominium would usually not wish to buy into a building with other medical practitioners in the same field. Initial business associate selectivity would often seem to have reasonable basis. A condominium may well get off to a better start if the other participants are known and are satisfactory to most other firms which will share in important decision making.

In the concept of preselection of unit participants, the commercial condominium perspective is quite different from that of the residential development. In a residential condominium, the purchaser in new construction uses price scales and the surrounding area in determining the type of residents who probably would be attracted to live there as his new neighbors. Rarely, except perhaps in ultraluxury accommodations, does the purchaser consider in depth the social and financial status of particular co-buyers. He leaves such matters to the developer and the bank which must grant mortgage loans.

The choice of participants is more urgent to many commercial unit purchasers. Special internal construction costs, the placement of equipment, the establishment of a known address, the hiring and moving of employees, the expenses for signs and other expenditures of a major nature would result in huge losses if immediate termination of ownership occurred. The requirements of other owners may inordinately increase costs of common charges to others; the business of others might seriously impair the comfort of one's own employees and firm; the activities of others might unreasonably add to physical depreciation of the entire property; the very character and stature of a building complex might be adversely affected by the activities of a single unit owner.

The credit rating and business history of a commercial or industrial firm are often readily accessible. The reputation of co-venturers for responsible business operations may be expected to be checked by careful participants before entering the condominium commercial agreement. Although many firms joining the condominium will not wish detailed internal finances to be disclosed to outsiders, some minimal credit information, available through ordinary sources, should be maintained by the developer's staff for discussions with serious prospects seeking condominium units in the same business complex.

Notably, there has been little mentioned about preselection in the advertising material offering business condominium units. But one can expect, as the author knows has been the case in particular instances, that prospective purchasers will want to know: Who are the other firms or persons going into this, and what can you tell me about them? Whether the developer likes it or not, he may expect prospective buyers to contact directly those who have already purchased units to discuss background and motivation. One way in which developers and partici- pants can both be protected from mere curiosity seekers at this important stage is by use of general rather than specific information.

Also, the offering might be limited to firms with a specific audited net worth as verified by a certified public accountant; or that has been in business for more than 5 years; or that has more than a specific number of employees; or that will be engaged only in one specific trade, profession or business; or that has a favorable business rating by a reputable credit inquiring firm. Whatever the formula attempted, the developer must realize that he is making a representation that might be heavily relied on.

It would appear that the type of business of other purchasers is one of the chief subjects of inquiry by prospective purchasers in building complexes serving more than one business or professional group exclu- sively. Picture the sad purchaser of a business unit in which he will be engaged as an interior decorator with a public showroom from which he also sells furniture. If two parking spots are exclusive for his business, with a large number of spaces open to common use by all owners and their customers, consider his later disgust to find out that an auto rental agency will be one of the unit owners. Just let the decorator's customers search for an empty parking space!

TIME FOR ORGANIZATIONAL MEETING

Another aspect of marked difference between residential and commercial condominiums is the organizational phase. Assuming, as is usually the case, that most units have been presold, first organizational meeting of the business condominium should preferably take place after conveyance of title, but preferably, if practical, just before the firms move into their new quarters. If the building complex is a conversion from rental status, the meeting should also take place just after title is transferred to the new owners by way of condominium. Some purchasers, fresh from land- lord-tenant relationships, still persist in individual negotiation with man- agement at this point in the same fashion of the tenant seeking arms-length help from a landlord's agent. Some, reflecting later on this attitude, realize that more effective action could have been obtained at a joint meeting by management with all participants. Also, there is the matter of friendliness and cooperation that can result from such a meeting.

Whereas residential condominiums have moving and start-up annoyances quite similar among purchasers, the business venture encompasses different business firms likely to have more costly, pressing, unique, and immediate problems initially requiring special management attention. Resident tenants can wait a few weeks until they are settled down before the first election and board meeting. Business condominium purchasers, however, have far too much at stake to wait that long to provide management with instructions for the business problems incurred through moving and start-up of their business, industry, or profession.

In the ordinary case, purchasers should insist that management call a meeting at the earliest possible time. This is practical when title to most units have been conveyed. If one or more important purchasers have not as yet taken title for only technical reasons, the meeting should include such firms as well, although no vote of a deciding nature should be permitted against the interest of these companies. In some situations it may be practical to hold only an exploratory meeting, with further business such as board election and policy being left for the immediate future when most firms taking the majority of space have taken title.

We may presuppose that many condominiums will be built so that separate moving will not burden other participants. However, in those cases in which commonly used platforms and elevators are to be used, the developer must himself prearrange an order of initial use which should be authorized by the management agreement, and which would forestall unnecessary arguments at the very outset of the venture. By meeting with purchasers, such problems will not be subject to mere whim and arbitrary solution, but rather by the real needs of respective purchasers.

TIME OF THE ESSENCE

The developer of commercial space experienced in the field knows that the timing for delivery and preparation of business units is underlined by financial pressures far greater than in the residential field. Businesses unable to relocate by planned dates may incur enormous costs brought on by delays and inconvenience.

"Time is of the essence" clauses are much more insisted on and obtained by business unit purchasers than when residential housing is offered. Developers are thus put under the burden of precise timetables, and they try desperately to include in purchase agreements some outlet for removal of timetable pressures. Purchasers, on the other hand, strive just as expeditiously to penalize the seller for any delays.

This crushing clock watching underlines all the more the need for the developer to presell as many units as possible before committing himself to a specific timetable for delivery. The authors knows of some proposed business condominiums that were not consummated because the slowness of sales discouraged the initial purchasers from continuing when the time for delivery factor remained unknown. As business condominiums become more popular, this problem will become less important.

LAST-MINUTE ADJUSTMENTS OF SPACE

As accurate as advanced planning may be, it is foreseeable that space requirements for purchasers may require minor adjustments before the taking of title by any unit owner. It is also possible that this may be done without prejudicing other purchasers if construction techniques and materials provide some flexibility for change. Sometimes, before conveyance other prospective owners may wish to contract for exchange or purchase of partial space obligated to others. Divisions of space in many business condominiums should be easily changeable if architects and construction engineers foresee problems of this sort. Such changes should be made before the filing of the declaration. Optimumly, the contract of sale should authorize minor changes without additional consent of all participants, which might be hard to come by. The aforesaid discussion presupposes that no unit purchaser's percentage ownership of common areas and maintenance cost obligation would be prejudiced by changes involving other unit owners. If such be the case, renegotiation of contracts will be essential.

EXECUTIVE LEVEL FOR BOARD SERVICE

If election of board members is by selection of title-holding unit owners, corporate or otherwise, it is difficult to provide the wording in the bylaws for the sensitive problem of the appointment of individuals to actually sit on the board by a selection made by the unit owners. Mere election may automatically result in the personal service of the top executive official on the premises; certainly a sole proprietor would wish in many instances to serve himself. Yet it may be expected that large firms, or divisions of substantial companies, will seek representation through appointed employees, sometimes delegating a seemingly burdensome task to a lesser employee.

The author has noted a general lack of attention to this problem in the organization and operation of the business condominium. This seems foolish when one considers that a board member is of little immediate help to management if he lacks the full authority to act as agent for his firm, or if he is hampered by personal inability to contribute meaningfully to the condominium management process.

Even a top management executive needs occasionally to seek a delay in important voting decisions until his company superiors or associates can review the consequences of proposals seeking his approval as a board member. But the lower down in line that the board member falls in company authority, the more often will meetings be interrupted and delayed by the need for board members to seek wisdom at a higher level of their own company authority. This problem rarely prolongs residential housing condominium meetings or decisions, but is a decided factor to consider when composing bylaws for commercial ventures. There will be times in many business condominium regimes when specific proposals legitimately will have to be typed and await the voting process for a day or more while company officials ponder their vote. This practice should not become a regular one, however, as would be the case if incompetent or unempowered persons were charged with board attendance and decision making by firms whose top executives chose not to take part in the management processes which the board membership contemplates.

One method by which the condominium could possibly help ensure competence in board members would be nomination and election of specific individuals, with prohibitions against assignment to underlings of board functionings. However, this practice may unnecessarily inconvenience firms with good management executives who are not top management. In addition, there could be a problem if some elected board members are top executives whereas others are far down the line of company status in other firms. If the board of directors contains such a mixed group, one can expect that top management will soon be replaced by subordinates. In applicable situations it may be possible to provide that each board member be either the sole proprietor, a general partner, a corporate vice-president, or the president.

The developer's attorney should try to draft bylaws that will work in this area for the particular companies and particular executives with which he is faced.

DAYTIME BOARD MEETINGS

Rarely are residential condominium board meetings held during daytime hours, but business condominium boards are just as likely to convene for luncheon meetings as during evening hours. It is best not to prescribe specific hours for board meetings in the bylaws, to avoid conflict on this subject at the very beginning of business. The copying of clauses from residential regimes has led to some rather foolish requirements for meeting times. If given discretion, the particular businesses, industries, and professions will accommodate themselves to convenient meeting times.

General membership meetings, annual or otherwise, also might be held during daytime hours if convenient. There too, the regime will not suffer from the residential condominium problems of working husbands who will not return before dark and who do not like weekends disturbed by condominium business meetings.

SUBSTANTIVE BYLAW TOPICAL CHECKLIST

PURPOSE OF CHECKLIST

The purpose of our review of certain topics below is to cull from ordinary bylaw provisions those of special importance in the business condominium, as well as to consider topics not ordinarily treated in bylaws and on which we should also focus when reviewing our subject.

Most declarations and master deeds of business condominiums have obviously been copied from residential housing forms, with rare exception. In fact, reading one of these documents in places with substantial numbers of business condominiums, such as Puerto Rico, you might suspect that the venture does not involve personal residential housing by the name given the condominium. Mostly the variations for conduct of commerce have been relegated to the bylaws of the particular business condominium. Perhaps this outlook is faulty, and the master document itself should provide more detail on the purpose of the venture. The likeliest reason for the declaration-bylaws arrangement would be the need for business flexibility, because the vote and mechanics for altering bylaws often are simpler formulas, requiring less than the unanimous vote regularly applicable to changes in the master declaration, as well as less operation of lender controls. Additionally, it has become customary to use the bylaws to cover many aspects of the business relationships for harmonious running of the commercial condominium regime.

Worldwide the condominium statutes give minimal direction for handling the special problems of commercial ventures, leaving the matter largely to the discretion of the draftsman of the major underlying documents. All too often, this draftsman has glossed over the problem by copying inappropriate residential housing language, or by omission of any formula for solution of expected business problems which must arise in the everyday activities of unit owners. In countries in which the commercial condominium is well established, business customs sometimes take the place of bylaw provisions. In the United States it is more urgent that bylaws be specifically addressed to important relationships.

Let us look at some of these problem areas, in the hope of obtaining a good starting checklist for achieving protective coverage of purchasers and more saleable units for developers.

USE OF SIGNS AND DIRECTORIES

The bylaws of business condominiums usually cover the problem of signs in one of four ways.

1. No signs are permitted to be erected or hung at various places, including the outside portions of the building facing the streets, without prior permission of the board of directors or managing agent or all unit owners. Usually guidelines for the granting or denying of permission are not provided in the bylaw provision covering this prohibition.

2. No signs are permitted to be placed within or outside a series of locations unless a general test is met. That test is often vague, such as one that the signs be "not inconsistent with the paint colors and structure of the outside of the building." Sometimes this permission is based on board or agent approval; other times there is no approval required from management.

3. In existing structures, as in a conversion, certain specific signs may be allowed to remain. In addition, in such instances the bylaws may or may not provide for replacements, additions, or repairs. In the latter cases, the approval of management may or may not be required by the bylaws.

4. The bylaws may make no specific mention of signs. There may or may not be a general decoration prohibition clause, one that requires prior management approval for inside or outside "decoration."

Most of the foregoing clauses are probably inadequate to avoid conflicts in the future. A sign over the entrance to a building adds enormous prestige to the tenant or owner named. A highly lit or large roof sign can ruin the sophistication and decor thought to be necessary by particular building occupants, and even decrease the value of a building. When considering bylaws on signs, the condominium developer should evaluate several important features applicable to signs.

1. The maximum size of the sign, whether it is to be short term and easily removable or of a more permanent material such as stone or metal, and the effect of the size of the sign on the specific location in which it will be placed, all should be considered.

2. The exclusivity of signs for certain owners may be important. Freedom for all owners to place signs may lead to the absorption of the advertising and prestige effect of particular signs by owners needing outside advertising.

3. The color of signs, as well as constituent materials, should be specified in detail.

4. Government regulation compliance should be the legal and financial responsibility of the sign owner. Nevertheless, it may be preferable on occasion for the regime to add the sign as a common element (even though for the exclusive use of one owner) because ownership would facilitate removal or correction of onerous or illegal signs. Moreover, any insurance costs applicable to the sign should be paid into the managing agent's escrow account, to assure payment. The law of liability for an accident caused by the sign might well depend on ownership. Whatever the determination of ownership and control, the condominium regime and all unit owners should be made additional assureds, to make certain that insurance covers this still vague area of liability.

5. Provisions should be made for the rights to place signs by business successors of original unit owners in the same or other businesses. Some reasonable method should be available for prospective purchasers to determine whether they will be allowed to employ signs, rather than waiting for later approval by the board after title has already passed. New owners may also be concerned about the right to remove their predecessor's signs, even if no replacements are sought.

6. A lobby directory board of all unit owners, or several directories, should be maintained by the regime as a common element, with control of the size of type, color, and contents placed in management. Let us remember that business directories may be quite limited, naming only firms and top executives, or be filled with names and locations of large numbers of company personnel. In tenanted buildings, additional charges are sometimes placed on tenants requiring large numbers of names and

locations on directories maintained by management. In the condominium, certain kinds of businesses may require such detail, as would be the case for a publishing house. Others may settle for less, as medical practitioners might, even if staffed by large numbers of attendants and nurses. Disputes in this area should not be encouraged by lack of attention to directories and the rights applicable to them, which should be thoroughly covered in the bylaws and be explained and understood by all condominium participants.

7. Parking and platform loading areas requirements may necessitate exclusive space reserved as part of some or all units outright or as a restricted common area for the exclusive use of one or more unit owners. Signs must be made, posted, and maintained for these areas, and the bylaws should adequately spell out responsibility here.

8. Approach signs are sometimes necessary on public or private roads nearby that must be traveled before entering the business condominium area. This might simply be a sign announcing the location of a building. It might also be a sign containing all or some of the names of the regime owners. A bylaw should authorize the board of managers to advertise on such signs, and spell out purposes and limitations.

USE OF LIGHT AND SOUND

Another area in which bylaws generally have demonstrated themselves to be deficient is that of use of light and sound. In reviewing this area, prior to decisions on a bylaw covering material, one should first thoroughly appraise the prohibitions of local government with reference to the use of light and sound. Moreover, especially with sound, there have been increasing enactments posing limitations in this area, and such government attitudes may be expected to intensify rather than be relaxed. The board of directors should have the right to pass on any new applications for permits or licenses for lighted signs or the use of sound equipment, rather than letting the bylaws merely provide their own prohibitions, possibly enforceable only after the fact.

Lighting provisions should include some of the following:

1. The bulb size and intensity of lighting fixtures inside and outside a unit should be specified if the effect will be felt by other unit owners and the general public.

2. The direction for focus of flood lights and similar items, which by themselves might not be a problem, except for the direction of focus, should be considered. For example, flood lights aimed at an adjacent

loading area might be acceptable, but the aiming of that type of lighting fixture at an adjacent building housing a different unit owner might lead to tension and friction unnecessarily.

3. It would seem important that the bylaws distinguish lighting fixtures in various categories: some may be used for safety or security purposes; some may be used to project or enhance advertising material, especially outside of the building; and some may merely be used for flair effects or mere decorative purposes. Each category should be treated separately, because the purposes are really quite unconnected and varying in importance.

4. The colors permitted for lighting are important. Sometimes a mellow or subdued color can take away the sharpness and intensity that might otherwise be bothersome to other owners or to the public.

5. The lighting in hallways adjacent to exclusive areas of unit owners should be covered in the bylaws or elsewhere in the building specifications, to avoid additional lighting requests being made by unit owners for commonly used areas.

6. There have been many studies made of the beautification effects of outside lighting on a building's appearance and its attractiveness to customers, the outside community, and the public generally. Often very ordinary buildings can be given enhancing decorative effects by careful outside lighting that takes advantage of green areas, shadowing, and coloring. Bylaws should give authority to the board here, but not to the detriment of any unit owner.

7. Provision should be made for the hours during which lights will be lit in commonly used passageways, entrances, driveways, parking areas, and other places necessary to be traversed by unit owners working later hours. It must be realized that some businesses will require regular or occasional use of their premises at hours past those ordinarily used for business by most other unit owners.

8. The nature and adequacy of wiring is probably more important for the commercial condominium for electrical uses, including lighting, than in the residential condominium. The residential condominium generally houses a standardized wiring system for the total complex or on a separate unit basis. However, the electrical wiring problem in a complex building unit is far more complex and will require immense variations to assure the adequacy of power sources for all purposes. If a unit owner must employ heavy-duty medical therapy or X-ray equipment or high-powered manufacturing equipment, the electrical workload capacity will depend on the adequacy of the overall electrical components, irrespective of the imposition of separate metering. The prospective unit owner should be assured of adequacy in special cases.

9. The location of circuit breakers and authority for control of this and similar equipment should be reviewed and set forth, so that simple electrical failures can be easily corrected by unit owners themselves, and major problems handled by management without confusion or danger.

10. The bylaws should also provide for emergency lighting problems that may result from power failures, including the responsibility for provision of maintenance and adequacy of such equipment.

11. Some condominiums have a traffic lighting system for internal operations. This may be in the parking area, on private roadways, on freight elevator systems, or elsewhere. Provision for timing and controls is another subject that may be important for unit owners and should be mentioned in the bylaws.

Sound equipment and machinery, as well as intensity use, should be covered in bylaw specifications, where applicable, to provide for some of the following problems:

1. The responsibility for insulation and diminution of sound where noisy equipment and machinery will be used.

2. Limitations on the use of loudspeakers and other audio equipment, including the ringing or buzzing to make the changing of shifts.

3. Limitations on the use of musical systems during working hours.

4. Sound limitations in meeting rooms, especially during demonstration or sales talk programs, and whether the equipment should constitute a common element.

5. The use of units or common areas for parties.

6. If private airstrips are used, any limitations on the types of aircraft, especially with reference to sound problems that may be disturbing to other unit owners.

USE OF DANGEROUS MACHINERY

Some business condominiums employ dangerous machinery, such as ultraviolet and X-ray equipment. In such cases, the bylaws should cover the responsibility for the utilization of detector machines within and outside of such units to prevent any dangerous situation from spreading.

A SPECIFICATION EXHIBIT

One choice might well be made at an early stage of drafting the bylaws for business condominium to simplify the documents. This can be done by annexing applicable specifications for technical operations in certain cases, attached as exhibits to the bylaws. This could be done for equipment to be housed within particular units, light, sound, and so on, without having to burden the bylaw paragraphs themselves with technical language. The bylaws paragraphs, however, should contain provisions and prohibitions that are important in connection with these specifications.

Consideration might also be given to paragraphs in the bylaws applicable to such specifications as "These bylaws do not prohibit any reasonable substitution of materials or equipment not changing the nature or extent of operations and not unduly interferring with business activities of other unit owners of the condominium regime or the nature and purpose of the condominium's structure or structures".

SECURITY

Each unit owner has his own security requirements, some with greater or unique demands. Yet, it may not be sufficient merely to obligate individual owners themselves to enlarged security measures rather than such costs being discharged via common expense fund charges.

A jewelry exchange may require its private guards to patrol entrances and hallways distant from physical plant, especially during evening hours. Adequate protection may thus mandate the patrol of areas that are commonly owned, and perhaps the placement of protective electrical devices in such locations. The bylaws, in covering unit relationships, should at least authorize board and management arrangements in this regard. Buying unit owners, especially those who are security conscious, should go into the details of protective arrangements that will be common responsibility, and thereby note what additional safeguards will be essential for their own firm's adequacy of protection.

One benefit of the condominium format thus might be the widening of opportunity for security. Many a firm owning its buildings outright has wished that neighboring areas and structures were patrolled, or at least provided with security devices. Such failures have sometimes increased protection costs excessively for single companies. Condominium arrangements might help solve this kind of problem.

For extensive developments, such as industrial parks, the bylaw documents should indicate whether entrance gate security will be provided, as well as patrols. Pilferage and outright large-scale stealing have become major costs of industrial production in many areas of the country. A substantial security force inside and outside of the development, maintained by common cost, with booths and gates as common elements, as well as incidental patrol equipment such as automobiles, may be an important feature of the planned condominium. Because of the substantial costs involved, this matter should be reviewed initially in the projection of services and costs.

VARIANCE OF DECOR

The nature and quality of materials used to decorate and cover hallways, entrances, and allied space may present a problem in business condominium harmony, if it is not solved at the inception of the regime. For example, some businesses lend themselves to attractive entrances, and may therefore insist on carpeted hallways and dimly lit entrances. However, if a less concerned unit owner shares the entrance, conflict may arise over the initial and replacement expenses for carpeting, wallcoverings, and so on.

In a residential condominium, there is usually considerable uniformity in decoration and use of entrance and hallway materials. However, this may not always be wise for the business condominium. If entire floors or buildings are singly owned and controlled units, there is less problem in figuring such needs as entrance and hallway materials. Sometimes it may be practical to provide that certain decorative materials for common areas be the direct expense of one or more unit owners, perhaps with the authority of the board to decorate or to pass on the adequacy or quality of decoration plans before replacements or repairs take place, and with the board to act in the event of a dispute.

It must be realized that on occasion the mere device of common charges, usually based on floor-space ownership, may create inequitable burdens on unit owners not requiring elaborate decoration, and who do not really share in the benefits of such approach. On the other hand, floors of office buildings containing several unit owners probably should be uniformly decorated in accordance with the kinds of businesses residents in the space. If radically different businesses are on the same floors, for example, medical offices and printing companies, decoration becomes a more complicated problem.

At the outset, decoration will have been directed by the developer. But he has left behind bylaws that will impose common charges for maintenance and repair. If clear marks of reasonable responsibility for needed decoration have been set initially, a great deal of later infighting can be avoided.

SELECTION AND USE OF MANAGEMENT

It is urgent in most instances that the condominium employ highly competent professional management to handle the problems of the particular professions, businesses, and industry which make up the condominium regime.

If separate large facilities make up each unit, or some units, there may be the tendency by unit owners to seek authority to provide a great deal of directly supervised private management to satisfy internal needs. It may be cumbersome in some cases always to have to rely on central management and its resident staff. Nevertheless, there will always be the need for board-directed condominium management to provide adequate coordination and to avoid disputes among unit owners.

The bylaws might give attention to the question of authority to give directions to the managing agent. Usually, practicality dictates that the board or its designee officer be the one to give general and specific instructions. It may, however, be feasible to allow private work to be done for unit owners when they bear responsibility for maintenance and repairs, especially in restricted common areas, so long as such activities do not remove the availability of the resident staff for work in generally used common areas.

Certain kinds of equipment, when commonly owned, requires a highly technical resident staff that must be supervised by a single person, if staff must service more than one unit owner. Bylaws may generally reserve authority for control to the board, including the right to allow an employee of one unit owner to represent the regime.

Emergency service availability may be more important in business condominiums than residential ones. Commercial and industrial equipment might cause local and large-scale catastrophes if developing problems are not noted and contained. Management of the condominium should make the rounds regularly to assure the safety of all participants. Studies on the adequacy of heavy-duty fire and sanitary equipment should be required where essential. Bylaws should adequately authorize the board to act regularly and promptly for such purposes.

The bylaws should provide for the powers of unit owners with reference to management selection or contract termination. Some owners will insist on the right to veto board selections of managing agents. Sometimes they may settle for a required high percentage vote of all unit owners, rather than merely the board, with adequate prior notice to members of the experience and qualifications of the proposed new agent.

It is not the general practice to place in the bylaws many provisions on managing agent duties in residential or commercial condominiums. At best, even in full-disclosure states, the management agreement is available for perusal. At worst, and in most jurisdictions, the management agreement is not executed or exhibited until the culmination of sufficient sales to assure creation of the condominium regime. This practice often leaves as blind items many of the key responsibilities of the managing agent, sometimes to be controlled by the developer. Moreover, the board of managers may later renegotiate or amend the agreement with wide discretion.

To forestall failure to require management services for unit owners, certain major management duties should be made mandatory contractual requirements by force of the bylaws, which ordinarily should not be changeable without an overwhelming unit owner vote. In this connection, the bylaws might include minimum requirements for such matters as:

1. Reports (business and taxation) which must be issued to unit owners and the annual or other periodic dates by which they must be sent.

2. The location and times of availability of the books and records of the regime for perusal by unit owners or their appointed representatives.

3. Duties by management to promptly cooperate with unit owners in issuing pertinent information and obtaining necessary board review and registration applicable to the sale, assignment, or rental of units by owners.

4. The limiting of the term of any management agreement, especially if the developer controls the initial firm retained.

CONTROLS ON BUSINESS ACTIVITIES

It is not uncommon for more traditional business associations, such as the partnership, trust, corporation, and joint venture, to specify in formative documents the chief purposes and direction of the business venture, sometimes severely limiting the scope of such activities. Because such firms traditionally are considered as single operating units in the eyes of the public and the law, irrespective of the number of employees or financial investors, the internal group or representative restrictions set on business product direction, marketing, and incidental operations are rarely considered as restraints contrary to public policy. However, if each of the participants were to suddenly become separate proprietorships or entities, any agreement of common business purposes or joint endeavors would smash against the torrent of court decisions enjoining unfair competition and unlawful restraints in trade.

Into which category will restrictions in bylaws of business condominiums fall? Business condominiums are usually co-ventures in only limited form, for convenience in sharing certain common benefits to operate independent businesses with greater economy and efficiency. Thus they are likely to be, and should be, considered as units that are separate businesses, subject to antitrust and similar restrictions when any agreements or combinations by co-participants aim at curbing competition or are otherwise coercive restraints in trade.

However, there are many types of agreements of restriction in American business that have been continually upheld and which may not fall into so perilous a category. The contract of sale of many businesses in the United States typically will include restrictive covenants barring the seller from further operating a similar business within a specified radius of space and time. Courts of equity have favored such agreements as protective against attempts at unfairness by the seller who might, in the absence of such a bar, eliminate the value of what he has sold by competing immediately against the buyer for the same customers.

Even while much of traditional zoning law still stands, upholding use restrictions on land (although with sharp arrows piercing at many long-held concepts), boiler plate clauses in purchase and sale agreements throughout American business regularly seek to protect new owners from incursions by sellers and others that could prove competitive disasters from the start, or just plain uncomfortable. In the future, new statutes and court decisions may alter some accepted principles in the latter field, but we may expect to see businessmen fight fiercely for preservation of certain basic protective concepts. It is likely that co-owners of realty who engage in businesses on their owned property will argue that initial and lingering contractual business restrictions on kinds of business use of realty by owners constitute primarily a chosen path for investment and an equitable safeguard against sharp dealings by associate owners, and not unfair competition or unlawful restraint of trade. In other words, the choice of business venture and risk of capital require some guidelines for protection of one's investment.

Noting from the very beginning the sensitivity of any business restraint to constantly widening statutory prohibitions, let us examine the varieties of protective restrictions on business use that the condominium business unit purchaser might consider for inclusion in bylaws to protect his capital investment.

First, let us view the problems posed by the builder or developer of the condominium who remains within or near the regime to conduct his own business activities. The developer may reserve one or more units for himself, for direct operations or lease to others. This may be by full ownership or by leasing units or common element space from the regime. In other instances, the developer may own space adjacent to the condominium complex which exists as built property, or on which he plans to construct business structures that may house his own business enterprise or be rented to others by him.

The purchasers of business units presumably will wish to restrain the promoter from overreaching by acts that would lessen the value of their purchased units. In that connection, one would expect the attempt to limit the nature of business activities in owner-controlled space within or near the condominium regime. Restrictions of this type probably are governed to a large extent by established law applicable to ordinary purchase-sale restrictions whereby sellers are barred from unfairly engaging in similar businesses that would jeopardize the value of the sold premises. Condominium owners, however, may wish to go one step further and seek authority to pass on the credit standing and general reliability of any of the developer's lessees, or sublessees, and so on.

The developer, on the other hand, may not want to be severely limited as to use of his own space, and he may try to fight off attempts to dilute his power and discretion to choose businesses and lessees. Experience has shown that the developer usually can retain wider choice in condominiums that are fairly large and that contain many varieties of business activities. In smaller developments, cautious buyers generally insist on more restrictions.

What about the unit owner's own assignees to whom he wishes in the future to sell his unit? Also, what about the choice of tenant by the unit owner who later decides, for one reason or another, to rent? In viewing bylaw restrictions on these transfers, the unit owner must realize that they may work for *or* against him. While he owns his unit, he may wish to pass judgment on the choice of another's tenants, or be assured that only a single business activity can take place in any unit. But, once he himself decides to sell or leave, such restrictions may limit the unit owner in achieving greater value or income from his unit. Thus it is important that restrictions on business activity be fair and equitable from both points of view.

Business condominium documents can and do provide different approaches to limiting unit owners to specific forms of business activities.

1. Sometimes an entire building is narrowly limited as to use. Such may be the case for professional offices solely for use of licensed medical

practitioners. Bylaws should provide clearly the intent and purpose of these limitations.

2. Some limitations are by floor rather than by unit. A building with two floors may be converted to condominium with the provision that the first floor be used only for a restaurant and the second only for offices. It may be good practice to have the bylaws give the reasons, for example by stating that offices will not disturb customers and operations below by noise or otherwise, whereas any more-active business, such as manufacturing or industry, will seriously impede the value of the premises below.

3. Some limitations are by unit. Most of these restrictions appear to be rather general, such as for "office" or "commercial" use, or similar phraseology that is general enough to mean many possible things, and probably make for disputes later. European and South American business condominium documents often refer to a specific regime purpose or *destination* (as in France) or *destino* (as in Brazil). Some American documents broadly permit use of units "for any lawful purpose." In the latter case, the draftsmen either did not concern themselves with use priorities, drafted the documents before units were sold, or relied on probable continuation of initial uses.

4. Some limitations are by building. If the condominium is a complex of separate structures, consideration is occasionally given to limiting the purposes of entire buildings. At times this is done to prevent nuisance operations, as would result from heavy polluters. Industrial parks and similar developments in which retail showrooms or outlets are not contained on premises do not present competitive problems as fierce as would be the case for a condominium shopping center.

5. Sometimes limitations are found in bylaw provisions giving the right of first refusal or approval to the board of managers or other unit owners, usually without specification of standards for the exercise of such reserved rights.

In many states it is the conclusion of realty attorneys that a total right of approval in the condominium board as the condition for transfer of fully owned units would violate real property rules, usually statutory, that bar unreasonable restraints on the exercise of the full power of alienation of real property by owners of fee title. Such is probably not the case with respect to approvals of new lessees or sublessees, because of the distinction in the type of ownership, at least in some jurisdictions. For these reasons, many condominium documents almost automatically confer a right of first refusal in the board, a right to have preference to buy, which is generally not considered as violative of alienation prohibitions. Rights to approve lessees and sublessees, not usually considered as barred, generally are conferred in boards of managers of condominiums, commercial as well as residential.

It would seem better practice also to place specific or general prohibitions on the use of property in the original declaration or bylaws, together with a short statement or explanation of the need for such limitations. This procedure may ward off later arguments about restraints in trade and arbitrariness in the exercise of the rights of first refusal and approval.

In commercial condominiums, unlike residential ones, the documents may place the aforesaid rights occasionally in one or more unit owners, rather than in the board generally. By such a device, a set of preferences may be initially established in the bylaws or declaration, whereby first choice for purchase or use of units about to be offered to others would be conferred on preferred unit owners. These owners may need the space for expansion, or for protection against other use of premises. By providing for such rights in the original condominium documents, valuable opportunities for widening business operations may be preserved. Some owners may wish to buy other units for the later purpose of expansion, temporarily leasing them in the interim period.

Take the example of a condominium industrial park. The prospective purchaser of a major structure may wish the right of first refusal for two adjacent buildings to be bought by others. The other owners may at the same time want the concurrent and reciprocal right of first refusal for the units holding similar rights applicable to their units.

A doctor owning a unit in a medical building condominium should consider obtaining the right of first refusal for immediately adjacent space. In later years, his expansion problems might be satisfied by such expansion. In addition, he may be interested in the additional space for investment purposes, that is, to rent the extra space to other doctors for income purposes.

Bylaw clauses should cover carefully the order of preference in which unit owners are themselves given rights of first refusal or approval. Contiguity that is vertical or horizontal would seem a reasonable basis for conferring such rights. Or, similarity of business or professional activity may be another standard. Not all businesses need contiguity of all operations. For example, a spacing of units in a warehouse condominium with a wide common loading platform might not be too burdensome; such procedure could prove preferable to taking additional warehouse space some miles away.

Initial unit owners who intend to lease immediately should be wary of bylaws requiring board approval, especially if their purchase is part of a package transaction, involving a long-term valuable lease to another firm.

METERING OF UTILITIES

The metering and discount practices of local utility companies will determine cost-saving procedures that might be invoked by unit owners. A typical decision will be whether to arrange for separate metering and service for individual unit owners, or alternatively, to secure single overall service and metering with internal billing arrangements to be made by the board of managers. One should review the condominium regime's administrative workload and convenience factors before using the last procedure. The cost of internal metering might not make that method worthwhile. One of the difficulties presented is the need for monthly billing of unit owners, who might otherwise be paying common charges and other costs to the board on a quarterly or other periodic basis. Monthly administrative costs for internal utility billings could cut deeply into any benefits from single metering of the entire condominium.

There is no reason, however, why two or more of the unit owners could not plan for joint metering arrangements for commonly used equipment operated solely for their benefit. Whatever the metering program contemplated, the bylaws should allow reasonable use of condominium flexibility to cut through ordinary restrictions on cost-cutting devices, so long as the procedures are consistent with independent ownership of units and joint use of common areas and equipment.

Because of the major cost involved, unit purchasers may hesitate in allowing the board to retain authority to determine metering of utility services, at least without individual owner right of veto.

RESTRICTED COMMON AREAS

Restriction of portions of common elements for the exclusive use of one or more owners is a much more usual procedure in commercial condominiums than in residential regimens. Nevertheless, many governing documents, including bylaws, do not adequately contemplate this special feature. It would seem that too much is taken for granted in the use of common areas; the layout of units and buildings is such that exclusivity is almost a necessity in many situations in which condominium documents have remained unreasonably silent.

Another problem applicable to restricted areas rarely treated adequately in bylaws is the method for converting a generally used or useable common area to a restricted common area solely for the exclusive use of one or more unit owners.

RESERVES FOR IMPROVEMENTS

One of the most disregarded subjects in business condominium planning is the method of providing for future major repairs and improvements that require heavy outlays of funds.

The more self-contained the individual units, the less the problem presented. But some condominiums in later years will run into such common expense burdens as replacement of elevators, reconditioning of heating and plumbing systems, rewiring of extensive areas, or new structural needs (such as employee recreational areas or swimming pools). How is the money to be collected?

The simplest but most onerous means for raising funds is to assess unit owners when the funds are needed. This simplest of methods may be impractical because of unwillingness or inability of some or all owners at any particular time to part with such large amounts of cash suddenly. Financing may prove difficult, although joint personal or corporate undertakings on loans by reliable businessmen may be adequate, even if state laws bar placing liens on common elements. Nevertheless, it is dubious that all the then existing unit owners would always agree to such procedure.

Preferably, some system of accumulation of reserves for contingencies and specific improvements, and the right to borrow for repairs and improvements, should at least be authorized by the bylaws. Consideration should be given to holding reserves in the name of individual unit owners, even if placed in the hands of a trustee, to avoid the income tax consequences that may result if the board is considered to be holding such additional funds as surplus income beyond expenses at the end of any taxable year. It should be pointed out that this area of the tax law has not as yet been adequately defined. It is hoped that the Treasury Department will realistically not view such reserves as taxable income to the board or unit owners, considering that unit owners are merely setting aside their own money as reserves for future expenditures.

Lending practices by financial institutions for major improvements to common areas will likely be more defined in the future, especially if statutory enactments clarify the availability of security for loans. If a condominium can obtain unanimous consent to borrow for such purposes, one possibility is the formation of a separate corporation to go on the loan, with or without the guarantee of the unit owners corporately or personally.

The widest possible authority should be granted to the board in bylaws to authorize such borrowings under any reasonable formats now possible or that will open as the result of new statutory enactment.

CONDEMNATION OF UNITS OR COMMON AREAS

The bylaws should provide the formula for allocating funds payable by government agencies taking condominium property under the right of eminent domain. It would seem that silence in the documents would be a severe oversight, because of the immense stake in the issue that unit owners would have.

First let us distinguish between two kinds of eventualities, each of which poses quite different problems. In one case, it is essential to have bylaws that provide for payments received on the *total* taking of the entire condominium property. In the other situation, probably more usual, provision must be made for *partial* condemnation, whereby only segments or edges of the condominium regime are eliminated.

The net effect of many documents read by the author, and used to establish business condominium regimes, would be to award a total condemnation payment on the basis of unit owner percentages in the common elements. This method of allocation might prove fair in residential housing in many cases, but this sort of formula fails miserably to take into perspective factors unique in business property regimes. Because of their proximity, similar design, and single purpose, it may be expected that most units in a solely residential condominium will have increased or decreased in value by close variations. If the initial common interest percentages were assigned on basis of relative original value, there would ordinarily remain a value relationship considerably related to the original established variations. Such continuing result can by no means be assumed for the commercial condominium.

In many, if not most instances, the percentage of interest in common elements for the business unit owner will depend either on unit floor-space ownership or on an initial approximation of value of his purchased space as compared with other owners. With the passage of time, much of the increase or decrease in realty value and business value of each unit will depend on business success, the build-up of location value, the success or failure of neighboring businesses, and the changing use of premises for particular product or service development. It may well prove intolerable, on the public taking of the entire development, merely to allocate proceeds based on the original formula for determining payment of common charges, voting, and the implementation of other rights.

One may argue that a formula for condemnation payments in a business condominium is therefore an impossible task on inception of the regime. Also having validity is the argument that draftsmen would be excessively burdened with the problem. It is therefore suggested by the author that a means for independent appraisal or arbitration be set by the bylaws, to dispose the problem equitably if the eventuality ever occurs. Preferably, some standards could be pronounced in a condemnation clause. It must be remembered that, in the absence of special agreement, the "just compensation" will be based on the value of real property being taken. Whereas courts generally deny payments other than for such a purpose, contractual arrangements among participants may be made for the sharing of such proceeds.

The bylaws should also give attention to partial takings by eminent domain. These may be of several varieties. A minimal condemnation of part of common areas could occur. For example, a municipality may wish to place a traffic light and island on the edge of condominium property. Obviously, if no one unit owner suffers property value loss to any substantial degree, the funds might be allocated in proportion to common interest ownership or under another simple method. If only a single unit is taken by condemnation, it would seem justifiable for that owner to receive most or all of the award, subject to the loss that might ensue to the regime by removal of the unit. Bylaws should provide for such eventualities.

One can foresee confusion and vexation if eminent domain removes restricted common areas that are vital to only a few condominium participants. If a great deal of the value of condominium sharing is based on such considerations, then the contractual documents should specify the method for allocation of damages in such instances, insofar as practicable.

Apropos to this topic is another important aspect. Bylaws should provide for the vote necessary to terminate the regime once a specific percentage of condominium property has been taken by condemnation. Continuation of ownership in condominium form might become impractical, either for lack of needed facilities or from the nature of use made of the condemnated space by the government unit seeking to utilize the property.

Most important, draftsmen, attorneys, and other counselors of the purchasers should consider the possible problems that could occur someday if condemnation comes about, irrespective of the unlikelihood of such occurrence in the near term. If adequate machinery is placed in the bylaws and the declaration to guide solutions, the condominium will face such problems with a workable structure for finding solutions.

HOURS FOR SERVICE: HEAT, AIR-CONDITIONING, CLEANING

Uniformity of servicing of units may not be practicable in a business condominium containing different kinds of enterprises, or even one with similar activities, such as an office headquarters, in which business demands require different scheduling of work forces, early or late shifts, and possibly around-the-clock activities for some owners.

Cases abound in which tenants in office buildings sign leases calling for services "during ordinary business hours," or "regular working hours," and then find to their chagrin that air conditioning or other comfort controls are shut off at five or six in the evening, even when business necessitates the firm working until nine or ten o'clock. If the condominium business unit is not self-contained with respect to heating and air conditioning, then bylaws should clearly specify that services applicable to the respective unit should be made available, or kept ready for availability, if this is an important requirement for comfortable business operations.

A building with radically different professions or businesses will more likely be troubled by this type of problem. Not only is comfort an issue for those requiring service beyond ordinary working hours, but a wearisome concern may arise in those firms who work the ordinary 9-to-5 workday. If common charges pay for utility or maintenance costs applicable to such services, then even the regular-hours firm must review bylaw and maintenance cost allocation procedures to assure fair and equitable distribution of costs, to prevent overcharging for the benefit of others. Much will depend on the developer's wisdom in building or dividing units in a fashion that can minimize problems of this sort.

Internal cleaning, window cleaning, and floor waxing in buildings with simple office units should not present too difficult maintenance and cost allocation problems, although more extensive units will require a higher cost load. Rather than making this item a common charge determined by percentage ownership, it may be wiser sometimes to provide for direct payment by unit owners, or for collection of special charges by the managing agent that would not be considered as common charges as otherwise defined. The benefits of a single building discount could thereby still be obtained.

There is no reason why management of the business condominium cannot conveniently collect regular cost assessments based on actual cost if it is not practical to collect them under the common charge formula. This procedure should be considered for bylaw insertion.

QUORUMS

When we speak of a quorum, we are talking about the number of members of a particular group whose physical presence is required at meetings as a condition to the legality of voting and decisions taken by such group at a specific time.

For annual or emergency unit owner meetings called for such important matters as the election of a board of managers, the necessity of adequate participation by large numbers of owners should be obvious. Because of the weight of decisions to be made, some unit owners would prefer full attendance. In a small regime, say with less than twenty owners, a high attendance requirement would seem logical. However, a bylaw always requiring 100 percent attendance as condition for voting would, in effect, give a veto power to any single unit owner who chooses not to attend because of a subject open for vote. In most cases, the bylaw requirement for quorums in business condominiums for annual meetings for owners appears to be an actual or modest majority, such as 51 or 60 percent. So long as adequate notice is given all owners, this may prove quite sufficient in many cases. In setting bylaws on the subject, a great many possible arguments are encouraged by lack of attention to such eventualities as vacant units; the right of lessees to substitute for owners, especially when they hold long-term net leases; and as we have discussed previously, the manner of selection of the representative of the owner. Most important, and quite different from residential regimes, the right of owners to send representatives with voting power is essential, unless the regime could reasonably and without inconvenience operate otherwise. In these days when even professionals such as doctors and lawyers incorporate, it would seem that such a representative clause is almost an absolute requirement.

The quorum for board meetings is another key matter for review. The number set for attendance is as important as the decision on whether to make such number absolute or not. Thus if the bylaws require a quorum of 60 percent of board members, the question remains as to whether this means that percentage of the total board that could exist or that does exist. If several vacancies occur, this problem sometimes gets sticky. For this reason, the bylaws should specify with precision exactly what the intent is here.

OPENESS OF BOARD MEETINGS

In the large condominium in which the board must be representative, there is still one way for membership to be kept closely aware of board activities without overloading the board with total membership. This method is the right of all unit owners to attend all or most board meetings. The additional right of all members to be heard on a variety of topics at such meetings could also be spelled out in the bylaws, even if such comments would only be advisory rather than of specific voting significance.

Such rights would be of little value unless the full membership of the regime were given copies of all notices of meetings sent by the secretary of the board to other board members.

MANAGEMENT PRESENCE AT BOARD MEETINGS

It would seem advisable for the bylaws to be at least permissive on the question of allowing the managing agent to be present at board meetings, as well as executive meetings in which the board has appointed an executive group to assume closer management responsibilities. The exception would be meetings at which the management agreement is scheduled for discussion.

This presence may be conducive to effective functioning of the condominium for several reasons. The secretarial function of sending notices, taking minutes, writing reports, and notifying members of joint action are tasks requiring professional expertise. In addition, one cannot expect busy businessmen or professional practitioners to spare the time for such technical functions.

At meetings there is often a need for specific information on current condominium financial and business status, as well as information on conflicts that may arise among members, or claims made that are based on assertions of alleged facts. It is the managing agent who would in the ordinary course of events be expected to aid in such matters. And, of course, in the preparation of budgets, and the exercise of the right of first refusal or approval of new entrants, the managing agent would be expected to prepare presentations for the top governing bodies that would lead to decisions in a reasonable and efficient manner.

ALTERNATE BOARD MEMBERS

Another problem that should be covered by bylaws relates to the election of alternate board members when vacancies occur on the board of managers or directors. Different draftsmen quite arbitrarily set different rules to apply on such occurrence.

Sometimes alternate board members are elected at the same time the regular members are elected, with an order of priority to serve in place of others on the happening of certain contingencies. Another method is to have an election for new board members as vacancies occur. Sometimes the election is by total vote of the entire condominium, and at other times the election is by the remaining members of the board themselves for the duration of the respective terms.

This matter is not a simple one to handle, because of the importance of real representation of all interests in the business condominium. A full review should be had of the effect of any system of this sort, to assure truly democratic representation and efficient operation of the business condominium.

BOARD PROCEDURE LIMITATIONS

The procedures for calling meetings, stating agendas, electing a chairman and committees and executive officers, supervising the managing agent, passing on new investor financial responsibility, as well as other obvious functionings are similar to other business entity operations in *form* but not in the *goal* of operations.

The business condominium board, as well as its appointed executive officers, function in a much more confined and unique sphere than ordinary business executives operating total businesses. Condominium management must seek ways to promote harmony among various independent businesses, as well as administering commonly used areas for the benefit of those same businesses. Bylaws should clearly spell out the goals of management, to prevent overreaching, and to set the basis for settling disputes which may arise. Prompt, fair, and equitable treatment of all unit owners, consistent with the purposes of the condominium, should be expressly mandated in the bylaws as the specific duty and obligation of the board.

Unlike the bylaws of single business corporations and other business firms engaged in their own enterprises exclusively, the business condominium bylaws must emphasize prohibitions against board action, just as importantly as containing authority for affirmative action.

For example, some companies purchasing units may wish prohibitions placed on condominium officials that would prevent their invading fundamental business privacy. They may seek clauses on management barring the board and its agents from examining the books and records of unit owners, or otherwise probing for production information or future individual company plans. In this connection, some firms may not even want condominium cleaning personnel on their premises at all, or at least not without supervision.

Let us not forget that one preference factor in favor of condominium is the avoidance of profit sharing and business disclosure that emanates from use of the common percentage lease in many forms of business tenancy. Many unit owners should consider insisting on bylaw prohibitions that would assure the confidentiality of particular business operations, so long as they are consistent with the purposes of the condominium venture and do not interfere with other owners.

EXPANSION OF THE CONDOMINIUM REGIME

For several possible reasons, including indecision on the receptivity of this new form of ownership, a developer may not wish initially to build more than a small number of units, holding back the use of some vacant land or adopting flexible construction programming. A prospective unit purchaser should be wary of declaration or bylaw clauses providing for an expandable regime, and be circumspect with regard to documents totally silent on the topic.

As the residential housing condominium form has developed, we have witnessed more and more attempts to construct in stages, without the final number and quality of units disclosed to original buyers. One can expect that developers will eventually pursue similar approaches when developing the business condominium. Financing may be more difficult for originally large groupings. Reservation of land may allow for more profit opportunities after the original regime is completed.

The business unit owner should be concerned about expansion for at least two reasons, both of which have little reference to the more tested residential housing condominium.

If the business regime is expanded beyond its original form, the entire atmosphere conducive to the original decision to purchase might be thwarted. Unlike the mere addition of similar types of units that usually faces the residential owner when expansion takes place, the business owner has much greater difficulty predicting the consequences of expansion. For example, a total office condominium might suddenly have a steel mill added to it physically and legally. The usual zoning valve will operate as less of an impediment to radically different uses than for residential housing.

We have already discussed the importance to purchasers of learning the nature of enterprises to share in condominium ownership. Expansion of the regime for new businesses, without the planning or consent of existing owners, can remove many of the reasons for buying in the first place. Thus the inclusion in the declaration or bylaws of reserved authority of the developer, without unit owner permission, to expand the condominium by construction of new units and amendment of the master documents, can pose serious problems. Such power should not be permitted to remain in the developer, unless the unit purchasers really have considered the matter and do not object.

Whatever the bylaw or declaration provisions applicable to later expansion, it may be fairer in many instances at least to grant to the original owners, or their representative board, the right of first refusal for later created units. Unfortunately, in many situations this right may be grossly inadequate and even futile. If the developer wishes to sell space to new businesses willing to pay exceedingly high prices for the new location, it may prove impractical for existing unit owners to match prices. Perhaps the right of *first choice of purchase* should be created, based on some maximum footage standard, rather than the mere right of first refusal.

The developer's reserved power to expand the condominium will be subject to the express and implied strictures of state condominium laws. Counsel for the developer should check this point thoroughly. Subject to such laws, there have generally been three different approaches to expansion.

1. In one type of relationship, the builder reserves the right to expand the condominium after conveying units, with the percentage ownership in common elements of each original owner to be contingent on the eventual act of expansion. In most instances in this category the decision to expand and the fixing of percentages definitively must be made by a specific outside date, typically 1 year from the date of filing the declaration and bylaws. Original unit purchasers would thus not be able to know the final percentage responsibilities for common shares, or even the extent of common areas to be created that will be subject to such charges. Especially when he engages in substantial undertakings, the business unit purchaser should carefully analyze the dangerous consequences possible from this approach.

2. At other times, the builder places in the declaration and bylaws easement, use, and right-of-way clauses barring the objection by unit

owners to *tie-in* arrangements with separate condominium regimes which the developer may be willing to construct later, usually on adjacent land, after completion and sale of the initial undertaking. In most cases, these agreements will amount to easement relationships for such purposes as crossing private roads or woodland, although sometimes they get pretty cloudy and complicated. By this device, the percentages in common areas held by original owners need not be changed; the builder has a longer time to decide to build additional units; and there will be less involvement in original owner affairs by purchasers in the expanded areas. If problems of cost allocation are created, they are regularly solved by creating a separate corporation similar to the residential homeowners association, with a formula in original documents for stock distribution and assessments for all affected owners.

3. The builder may reserve the right to build a *minimum* and *maximum* number of units, dependent on sales acceptance, but with the final decision to be made prior to conveyance of the first condominium unit. In most states, unfortunately, this special bit of information is just not adequately disclosed to prospective purchasers. The appropriate way to handle sales would seem to be by making available two or more schematic diagrams showing layouts and the sizes of common area amenities contingent on the completion of sales. An employee recreational area and swimming pool takes on a different character if used by 100 rather than 70 workers. Parking areas originally designed for 100 cars can get cramped when required to service 130 vehicles. If the developer does not represent the specific number of units to be built by making available condominium documents from the start, it is of moment to ask for representations before contracting.

INSURANCE COVERAGES: UNIT OWNERS AND COMMON AREAS

THE NATURE OF PROPERTY PROTECTION AND COST DETERMINATIONS

Relationships in the business condominium require that careful thought be given to a workable insurance program covering possible losses in value stemming from the ownership and operation of property in business condominium form. For example, it is not adequate to view hazard insurance in the same way a full owner of property does, or as does a long-term lessee. Certainly the condominium owner will wish to protect against damages to that property he owns in unit form for exclusive use, but, in addition, he must delve into the problem of protecting his undivided interest in common areas. Of necessity this means adequate coverage of the interest of all unit owners in all the commonly used property owned in undivided percentages by each owner.

It would also seem important to each owner that the other owners are adequately covered by insurance for the areas they own exclusively, because some of the value of each unit flows from the continued existence of the total condominium relationship and the benefits flowing from the common good of the regime. Hazard, liability, and related insurance coverages are of urgent importance in this connection.

Cost allocations by the board of managers for assessment purposes definitely present special challenges in formulating adequate and fair joint and intra-protective insurance programs. Business units tend to be, comparatively speaking, unique, especially when varieties of businesses are carried on in some regimes, necessitating inordinately unequal amounts of insurance coverages of all types, and resulting in charges different among participants. If insurance of many kinds is collected as common charges, the usual percentage interest in common elements method for allocation will often be immensely unfair. In some states, such as New York, the usual assessment method, by statutory authority, may be altered for excessive insurance costs; in some states this may not be possible. In the latter it is suggested that statutes be amended. (Here again we have a cost that possibly should be collected under the bylaws without making it a common charge item, thus permitting a fairer determination when a total condominium policy cost must be divided among members of the regime, as is the case with hazard insurance in some regimes. It would seem that the major problem would be reducing an unpaid charge to a judgment lien rather than the type of lien permitted by statute for unpaid common charges. Because substantial business personal property is likely to be on the premises, for satisfying unpaid debts for insurance costs, the absence of the additional right to foreclose a statutory lien on the entire unit and the percentage undivided interest might not be too difficult to accept.)

In addition, unit owners must concern themselves with possible damage eventualities because of service on the board of managers, a representative body covering activities of other firms as well as their own.

HAZARD INSURANCE

Before analyzing the adequacy of insurance coverage for condominium property, we must first determine who will be the policy beneficiary, for both payment of proceeds and eventual benefit from the application of those same proceeds.

Once we conclude, as often we must, that the entire real property of the condominium regime should be guarded by the board of managers, then it seems logical that insurance awards be paid to the board and disbursed to repair or rebuild damaged areas. The nature of condominium, both exclusive areas and commonly used space, necessitates overall protection of all realty. To permit separate policies for each unit might lead to confusion in payments for work (for example, when damage occurs to more than one unit and the common areas), unnecessary lawsuits among unit owners, and easy defenses among insurers for balking at payments. Each unit owner's interest is conditioned somewhat on a continuation of an existing, viable, and operating total condominium regime. Such factors mandate the rebuilding of damaged areas, irrespective of location or utilization, and such responsibility is ordinarily imposed by statute or the bylaws on the board of managers. To shoulder that responsibility, the board should be made the beneficiary of the fire and other hazard policies covering common areas and *all* units. In addition, the effects of ordinary loss payable clauses for mortgagee protection must be limited by subordinating such rights in bylaws to the board's discretion to rebuild, repair, and restore, with proceeds of insurance paid to the board as policy beneficiary.

This type of procedure has become standard in many states for residential housing condominiums, and is accepted by most banking institutions, although many insist on the additional vehicle of an insurance trustee (typically a commercial bank) that would be paid insurance proceeds on behalf of the board, with disbursement to be made in accordance with an agreed rebuilding schedule consistent with the bylaws, state statute, and original trustee agreement. It appears logical to apply this same thinking to commercial condominiums for the protection of all unit owners. The major difference in the insurance approach, however, must be in the method of fixing assessments for insurance cost, which we have already discussed. A procedure for accommodating the insurance problems of the separate participants, by collecting premiums based on actual cost, removes any argument against unfairness in board collection procedures, assuming that the assessments are determined on the basis of an informed insurance survey. Insurance companies competing for policy business here might be convinced to provide aid to the board in fixing costs among units.

Each owner, however, must also take out a separate insurance policy covering damages to such items as machinery, fixtures, furniture, and personal property, unless some of these items, especially permanently attached machinery, are determined as coverable by the overall hazard policy and riders. Such decisions depend on the nature of the condominium, the convenience to unit owners, and the availability of adequate policies that would give such coverage on an overall basis. Although personal property, such as furniture, is never covered in master condominium hazard policies for residential homes, the business condominium may sometimes require a different outlook. One greater difficulty than with residential units is the added responsibility of management to check on unit owner improvements and added market and replacement value of units that necessitate added coverage, especially to meet standards that would bar insurer defenses of inadequate coverage as related to value.

In an overall master hazard policy, certain endorsements should be included for the protection of the regime and its members.

1. There should be a waiver of the right of the insurer to subrogate against any unit owners, the board, or its members, and this should protect the employees and staff of all unit owners.

2. No act of insuring of any owner by other policies should diminish the right of the board to collect on the master policy.

3. Invalidity from acts of any of the insureds, employees, business visitors, or the managing agent should be waived, when the acts are beyond the control and direct knowledge of the board.

The master policy should permit board termination of the entire regime if an adequate vote of owners takes place as permitted by the bylaws and statute. Such a clause will prevent an insurer from demanding a right to repair or rebuild when its cost analysis indicates saving instead.

Provisions for essential notice should be included in the policy giving adequate forewarning to mortgagees of intended cancellation or other termination of the policy, with the same notification period given the named insureds. The policy should expressly name the board of managers as the insured, and better still, add all the unit owners by a group phrase, even though the bylaw procedure for payment necessitates that the board of managers receive all proceeds as the beneficiary.

LIABILITY INSURANCE

Liability claims arising out of occurrences involving the common areas should be protected by adequate liability insurance held by the board of managers, preferably in the names of the *board of managers and each unit owner for liability as a co-owner*.

Insurance companies have generally refused to issue master package policies covering both hazard and liability for all units as well as the common areas. This necessitates a separate board liability policy for the common areas, and separate policies for each owner applicable to liability growing out of his ownership and use of his own unit.

Care in each case should be exercised to cover employees and agents of the board and unit owners. With hazard policies, there should be no overlapping of policies that could present an argument of diminishment of coverage for a recalcitrant company at time of claim.

Cross claims by unit owners and their employees should be permitted under the board liability policy. In that respect the condominium regime would be treated as if it were a separate entity for claim purposes. A unit owner who smashes his car in a common area parking lot because of negligent placement of wooden beams in an unlit area by an attendant should be able to sue the regime, even though he himself is a co-owner of the parking area.

SPECIAL INSURANCE CONSIDERATIONS

Some rather difficult management problems may arise with business condominiums in connection with insurance coverage.

1. Some owners may insist on expensive extended coverage in the overall master policy, whereas others may not wish to pay the additional cost. A feather merchant may be most concerned about water damage, and therefore seek coverage in all available forms. If these expensive riders cover the entire condominium, other owners may be most disturbed. The solution to this problem probably rests with a separate assessment scheme, whereby separate riders for extended coverage could be issued for particular owner premises, without blanketing everyone with the same charges.

2. There is much more reason for the managing agent to examine unit premises for insurance protection than in residential housing. Insurance appraisers would be required to review property values and safety conditions in connection with insurance adequacy and company standards. Almost any form of physical examination might lead to tensions if not handled capably by competent management and insurance staff.

3. Developing concepts in *contingent business insurance* must be examined and adapted for practical and legal use in the business condominium. The value of other unit owners may, in certain instances, be important monetarily to other unit owners who share condominium interests. Whether a legal, insurable interest can be found to exist remains to be seen, and should be an interesting subject for further study.

4. Businessmen may be hesitant to serve on the board of managers without some form of major personal liability policy. Consideration should be given to a review of benefits that may flow from incorporating the common areas, whether necessitated by state law.

5. In many states the only form of title insurance policy available does not insure against damages that might ensue if the condominium was not validly formed pursuant to the applicable state statute. No title policy should be accepted by a unit owner without such protection. Otherwise the insurance only covers title to the underlying land, and not to the key real estate exclusively owned by condominium declaration as well as common areas other than land. Huge business investments should not be made without full title policy coverage.

INCOME TAXATION: THE REGIME, UNIT OWNERS

REGIME INCOME AND EXPENSES

In the residential condominium field, the Treasury Department in several instances has directly or implicitly recognized that the condominium format is merely an agency device for convenience of independent unit ownership. This has been stated to be the case even if the common elements are incorporated. Whether the same attitude will prevail for business condominiums remains to be seen, and we will have to be continually observant as new rulings appear, once use of this form of ownership widens in the business field. It would seem that a similar attitude would be reasonable, because the interim management of a condominium that collects common management charges, as well as covering expenses for operations of common elements, is not itself a profit-making venture in most cases, but merely a convenient device for covering income and expenses applicable to individual owners.

The business condominium does have a strictly commercial purpose behind it, unlike the residential form. Nevertheless, this factor should not preclude reasonable determinations of mere conduit treatment for the management aspects. Whether the corporate form would create more income tax problems than an unincorporated board of managers cannot be determined at this time and must await future developments. Because separate mortgages and real property tax expenses are paid directly by each unit owner, only a small portion of expenses flows to the management of the business condominium. It would seem highly unfair to cloak such payments, largely for common element maintenance, as indirect income to the payers themselves. If, on the other hand, the regime receives any sort of commercial income other than the aforesaid, such as from outside persons paying for special services, then certainly reportable income would exist. However, it would seem more equitable to allocate such income directly pro rata to each unit owner, rather than taxing the mere agent-conduit board of managers and their constituted representatives.

The alternative would be to tax the interim condominium government much like a merchant association typified by organizations of shopping center tenants. In such cases any surplus rental over expenses at the end of a taxable year would be taxable income (Internal Revenue Ruling 64-315). As a safety factor, therefore, the board of managers should strive not to possess such a surplus at the end of the year.

It is hoped that the Treasury Department will take a view consistent with reality and consistent with their position to date in reviewing residential condominium income and expense problems. If their view on any point constricts or inhibits the needed growth of this new form, then it is hoped that Congress will act speedily to correct the situation and permit the widening use of this new form of enterprise that encourages independent initiative and greater distribution of individual ownership and business control throughout American business.

THE INDIVIDUAL BUSINESS UNIT OWNER

Unlike the residential condominium unit owner, who is limited to the gratuities of Congressional legislation for such limited deductions as mortgage interest and real property taxes, the business owner is generally able to deduct all "ordinary and necessary" expenses involved in his profit-seeking enterprise.

Each business unit owner will probably be able to take deductions for depreciation based on his allocated cost, with the individual mortgage added to the basis on which depreciation can be computed under existing rates permitted by law. The depreciability of the purchase price, together with nonreal estate equipment, can be very sizeable in permitting extensive write-offs. In addition, types of business expenses otherwise allowable for commercial enterprises should ordinarily be permissible for the business condominium owner. Also, those amounts that are paid as common charges for management and upkeep of common elements should be deductible as pro rata expenses for operating commonly owned property.

In this case the board of managers should be viewed realistically as the agent-conduit for each independent owner.

If capital improvements are made through special assessments of unit owners, such as for a new heating system, it would seem that the rules applicable to capitalization of costs, rather than immediate deductions for expenses, would apply even though the purchase is made as an owner of an undivided percentage of the acquisition. Once again, we are relying on a realistic attitude in projecting tax responsibilities, and it is essential that at any particular time all persons concerned consult expert tax counsel for their then current views on applicable laws and regulations.

CHAPTER VI

INSTITUTIONAL AND SYNDICATION FINANCING OF BUSINESS CONDOMINIUMS

THE UNDERLYING PROBLEM FOR INSTITUTIONS

Perhaps the single, most important factor delaying widespread use of commercial condominiums has been stubbornness of lending institutions to enter the field. Much of the hesitation does not have a firm basis, and is nothing more than shallow thinking that in the past has sometimes discouraged new forms of financing and held back needed change on economic and social levels. Gradual increase in the number of condominium business loan inquiries and breakthroughs by more imaginative lenders in providing protective mortgage documentation may be expected before long to lead to innovative and profitable lending practices by many institutions in this and following decades.

As with any new concept that requires heavy stores of financing, decisions must take into consideration the myriad of problems in any analysis of business loans, and these should be confronted, understood, and then challenged by a practical business approach. The special aspects of condominiums must be weighed against applications for more conventional kinds of financing; to take advantage of this new form of ownership the lending institution must have reason to conclude that such an investment is equivalent or superior to others available. It is the feeling of the author, from conversations with bank officials, that many mortgage officers are sincerely interested in the business condominium, and are carefully following reports of financing attempts in their own and distant communities.

For better clarification of our subject, most of our initial discussion focuses on the mortgage loan for a permanent unit owner rather than in development and construction phases. Then we turn to the latter subject.

GOVERNMENT FINANCING: A TESTING GROUND

As yet there has been no substantial experience by most institutional banking and insurance companies with business condominium financing. Some of the larger condominium developments, especially industrial regimes, have been financed and even promoted through state or local government assistance agencies seeking to encourage community business development. By utilizing the condominium form, such agencies have been enabled to promote successfully the clustering of independent businesses, bringing together privately owned firms that might otherwise not locate in the particular community. An example is a printing building in New York City developed as a condominium regime with state financing aid in 1971, which has become a center for various phases of the graphic arts business, drawing individually owned enterprises as unit purchasers that might have moved away from or never located in that city. Although community development and renewal, rather than promoter profit, are the primary motivation of government sponsorship, the procedure is revolutionary in its selection of the condominium format. Obviously, the choice of condominium implies a decision that full, independent ownership of the firms involved should be extended to realty ownership as well by condominium, a method that tends to retain businesses in a community more than mere leasing. Companies being asked to resettle or remain in a locality often complain of offers that omit the guaranty of long-term operating premises maintained under reasonable charges.

Some of the formative judgment by government to aid in sponsorship of business condominiums would appear to flow from such reasons as:

1. The flexibility in arrangement or concentration of an enterprise that lends itself to urban renewal plans for the highest and best use of space.

2. The promotion of individual ownership that often gives competitive vitality to a business complex of single-industry companies.

3. The convenience to the public and other businesses resulting from a concentration of specialized enterprises at a single location.

4. Sudden concentrations of new industry tending to aid and create related supply, support, and distribution businesses in the same community and otherwise aid local flow of commerce.

5. The employment within a community, or the encouragement to relocate to the new industry area of specialized and general labor forces.

6. The stability of the location for the businesses and companies involved.

It is believed that large numbers of similarly financed developments will be financially encouraged by state and local government in the years to come, strengthening by exposure and experience the highly flexible business condominium form of enterprise. On the horizon loom vast industrial park, research, medical, and other facilities that will be government-sponsored as condominium regimes.

Local assistance programs usually emanate from special governmental authority agencies empowered to sell bonds or notes to the public to raise funds for urban development and local assistance. Because of the high rating and tax exemption of government-backed obligations, the rate of interest payable to investors on the bonds tends to fall considerably below market rates for ordinary business corporation obligations, either on commercial bond issues or on institutional lender mortgage loans. Thus the benefits of such low costs can help reduce the realty financing charges to individual firms seeking to locate in business condominium regimes.

Government agencies, in several instances, have already noted that they cannot preserve lingering management and decision-making control that they regularly exercise when promoting residential housing cooperatives and similar developments. Business unit owners demand their right to select and govern their own management to a considerable degree, whether their government aided in the original construction or issuance of purchase money loans.

Government agencies are sometimes staffed with persons inexperienced in an ordinary business enterprise, who make unreasonable requests for continuous control on ventures originated or sponsored by government. Often this attitude stems from fear of public exposure of any errors. Although each development is different, it must be assumed that the greatest, if not total, control of management ordinarily should be granted to the unit owners at the earliest possible moment. Lingering powers should be concentrated on vetoes applicable to all substantial mortgagees, which we discuss on later pages.

BANKING INSTITUTIONS: COMPARING COOPERATIVES

Thus far a substantial segment of bank mortgage financing in the business condominium field has been directed toward professional buildings housing doctors, dentists, and related professionals. Besides mortgage loans, the banks have also been interested in issuing business and equipment loans to starting or expanding professionals, largely based on the high credit ratings of their occupational group or individual past performance on prior loans.

This early emphasis on such occupations is perhaps a carryover from past years when there was occasional financing by banks of similarly occupied buildings developed under cooperative stock corporation ownership, the participants subscribing to stock and proprietary leases that evidenced their special and exclusive rights of occupancy. Loans to finance the cooperative corporation itself for construction or rehabilitation of older buildings were more easy to obtain, in the few instances of use of this form (especially if easily convertible to rental use), than funds for individual participants to purchase their stock on completion of the premises. One single overall mortgage would exist, secured by the entire structure or structures owned in the name of the cooperative corporate entity, paid for by carrying charge assessments borne by tenant-stockholders, payable regularly to the corporate owner.

Before the advent of the condominium in the 1960s, there was really little alternative to the cooperative business joint venture in realty ownership. Traditional concepts of real estate security, especially the idea of not going above a conservative percentage of appraised value, often did not permit financing that made cooperative business corporation development practical. There was simply no strong motivation to find a way to help develop real estate business ownership by joint venturing of independent firms seeking prime space for operations. With the widening search by institutional lenders for more effective use of funds in an expanding economy often plagued by capital shortages, this attitude has weakened considerably in many directions recently. The business condominium concept has arrived at a time when institutional lenders are demonstrating more imagination than ever in seeking well-secured but creative loans that achieve income and goals not always approachable under traditional concepts of real estate lending practices, especially in the short-term lending field. Changes loom as well for long-term lending.

There has been marked hesitancy by businessmen to be captivated by the stock cooperative venture, probably because of the tremendous burden for unpaid charges that result on default of other participants.

That is to say, if several large industrial companies are unable to meet their share of mortgage and realty tax obligations, the remaining cooperative stockholders must make up for unpaid obligations of others on those charges, such as property taxes and mortgage obligations, to preclude foreclosures that would void their own investments. On the contrary, in the condominium venture each unit owner is subject to a separate tax assessment and, usually, his own direct mortgage obligations. Defaults by others affect smaller maintenance charges that do not include mortgage and property tax payments, the omissions by others thus not falling with such weight on the remaining participants. For these reasons, an institutional lender making a mortgage loan to a condominium unit purchaser can focus principally on the credit of the proposed mortgagor and the value of the unit.

When we talk about cooperatives, we are not talking about business cooperatives that are common ventures such as in the dairy and farming industry, in which the stockholders are mainly engaged in a common business production or marketing enterprise and use the device as a pooling method for direct participation in a common business effort. Rather, the business cooperatives we have discussed are those in which the stockholders are owners of entirely separate and often unrelated businesses, utilizing the cooperative corporate form solely or mainly to own real estate and related properties conducive to more efficient or convenient operations of their independent businesses.

The idea of business corporate cooperatives for independent businesses sounds good, but it has never been actively pursued by lenders or borrowers because of bank refusal to finance the cash investment needed to purchase stock. The underlying mortgage for the total cooperative is a simple commercial mortgage that probably never posed great problems. But, practically speaking, a method that would not also provide financing for the cash purchase price of stock would be faulty.

The institutional lender faced with applications for unit condominium loans is faced with separately obligated borrowings by independent entrepreneurs for individually owned businesses, with the security for the mortgage loan being the unit together with an undivided interest in common elements. Ordinarily, by state or federal law or bank requirement, each loan would be a first lien, the most superior security possible in order of preference to creditors.

SAFETY OF LOANS

One of the features protective of mortgage lending in the business condominium field is the division of risk to lenders who give a substantial number of separate loans to purchasing unit owners. If instead of condominium, an entire building were the subject of a 10 million dollar loan to a single mortgagor who operates the structure on a rental basis to others, the lending institution enters an *all-or-nothing* situation as to possible default of the huge undertaking. However, if separate 500,000 dollar loans are each taken by several business firms with separate responsibility for payment, the risk of default is substantially lessened because of the division of risk. If a particular weakness develops because of any one unit owner, the ability of a mortgage lender to recoup losses and reduce any diminishment in the value of the investment is much stronger because of the division of ownership. Oftentimes, banks caught in defaults of huge sums on single-building mortgages must of necessity negotiate and delay foreclosure, must move conservatively to preserve some continued semblance of payments. With smaller obligations, defaults can be handled much more efficiently as to foreclosure, and decisions to negotiate or delay continued payments will have less of an effect on the total obligations coming from the same building.

It may be argued that single triple-A–credit-rated owners are preferable to the many mortgagees in a condominium building. But not every loan can be made to such distinguished borrowers. Tremendous numbers of middle-credit-rated firms exist in this country that regularly do business with banking institutions, many of which make large real estate investments involving mortgage loans. A cluster of such credit subjects in a single condominium complex, with division of risk, might be an attractive source for future banking and insurance company mortgage loan business, enabled by the condominium method of financing. Moreover, the future may be expected to find high- and medium-rated companies together in the same condominium complex, with banks wishing to make loans having little alternative but to yield to a new form of loan—the business condominium—to avoid losing good loan opportunities to competitors.

VARIATIONS IN MORTGAGE TERMS

Unlike residential buildings, business unit condominium mortgage loans may vary considerably among the different mortgagors. Interests rates, amortization payment rates, prepayment clauses, as well as the term of the loan may show wide differences in the case of borrowers in the same building, because of the larger variations in loan requirements and wider reliance on personal and corporate credit likely to be applied to commercial unit mortgages. This is especially to be expected if the occupations of unit owners vary widely.

One mortgage term that will be interesting to watch is the requirement for personal obligation on the debt by individuals. In many localities banks are willing to accept corporate business undertakings on business property mortgages, without adding personal liability, because of a high corporate credit rating or the safety of the realty securing the loan. There is really no justification for applying different standards for condominiums; once institutional lenders begin to accept the condominium unit as adequate security for mortgage loans, without adding personal liability if not otherwise required, we will be able to mark a point of acceptance that will move this new concept ahead in business thinking.

COMPETITION IN LENDING

Many prospective purchasers of business units will have already developed substantial credit lines with financial institutions before being faced with unit purchases. There is, therefore, a much greater likelihood than in residential regimes that unit owners will be able to arrange their own financing of mortgage loans. This could disadvantage the principal lending institution desirous of maximizing the number of loans throughout the business condominium. Good competitive initiative will be called for, a procedure that might bring welcome results to purchasers and establish a new bank with expanded business relationships with new enterprises for future purposes as well.

APPRAISAL FACTORS

The professional appraiser who is faced with an analysis and value judgment of condominium business units must not forego a thorough review of traditional factors going into evaluation of any business property mortgages. However, additional emphasis should be given to those matters especially significant for condominium properties, some of which might be overlooked by appraisers not having substantial experience in this field.

1. An area business study should be made that takes into consideration the current availability of commercial space in the locality under study. Localities and availability of business space of all types, however, must be viewed from the new condominium potential versus any competition.

Let us take one possible example to show the new perspective required. Many buildings accommodating warehouse companies are not located, because of prohibitive costs, close to business office centers. On the other hand, there are different companies in congested metropolitan areas that would be greatly convenienced by having some of their warehouse facilities close to their main business arteries. In the latter case, a high-rise condominium warehouse building centrally located could make possible immediate servicing of nearby parent companies, thereby relieving the problems created by the customarily long distance to substantial warehouse facilities. The appraiser must probe whether the condominium concept in this or similar instances would permit a result to be reached that has a value element not existing in other types of ownership. The appraiser should not merely weigh a market or reproduction value on such buildings against those distantly located.

Although the foregoing example explores only one possibility, distance relationships, the purpose of the example is to indicate to the appraiser that he must understand special advantages that might come from condominium ownership, as opposed to ordinary forms of property control or rental. Location may in many cases be an essential element that can provide available space in centralized locations not otherwise available by forms of occupancy other than condominium. Certainly if business firms consider ownership of space as a key element of their operations, then the value of the condominium concept often will be in the availability of better locations.

2. Square footage cost analysis should also include convenience and cost savings. Quite often a mere mathematical computation of the cost of space is made simply by taking the total cost of acquisition and dividing it by the square footage. Because many rental buildings and traditional real estate structures in the same community are basically similar in layout and use of space, such an evaluation is often helpful to the appraiser when comparing one building with another or one office with another. However, new condominium buildings or those that have been substantially rehabilitated may provide for unique layouts, the convenience of which adds essentially to total business operations that will reduce *operating* costs not disclosed by ordinary appraisal techniques. The appraiser of real estate would therefore have to study business operating essentials to determine the real cost of the use of condominium space. This aspect will be difficult for many professional appraisers not trained for profit-and-loss analysis of business operations.

3. Some buildings can never be comparable to others already in existence, and may present difficult problems in appraiser analysis. For example, a small community may suddenly have presented to it a new professional medical condominium where nothing of the like had ever existed before. Only the future can indicate the traffic in business and the value to doctors of location in this building. The appraiser, once again, would have to make an economic evaluation of the needs for the services in

the community compared with existing professional services located elsewhere.

4. Because business condominiums involve a complex of enterprises tied together by ownership in common areas jointly used, special attention should be given by the appraiser to the problems of parking and material handling. One of the difficult problems to be solved, to have a harmonious condominium complex, is that of the adequacy of entering and leaving the premises, whether by the parking of automobiles or by the delivery of materials such as inventories and supplies for business operations. Provision for unit owners, their employees and staff, as well as delivery trucks should be carefully evaluated by the appraiser. New construction that provides for different levels for loading platforms could sustain privacy and exclusiveness within the complex and is the type of development that we may expect in the years to come in business condominiums such as industrial parks and groups of manufacturing plants.

5. The appraiser should consider the question of expandability of the individual unit and the entire condominium. He should question the methods for solving the need for additional space by unit owners or by the entire condominium in future times. Clauses and bylaws, such as we have discussed, that allow flexibility are important to the appraiser. If a company is located totally within a condominium unit, it would be a severe hardship to relocate later for widened operations. On the other hand, if a company has only part of its operations within a condominium unit, the problem is less aggravated. The type of businesses and the layout of space are factors for the experienced appraiser to judge in this connection.

6. The appraiser often glosses briefly over future economic factors in traditional, comparative appraisals, but he cannot escape the subject when reviewing condominium unit values as security for a loan. By eliminating the lessor-lessee relationship, the unit purchaser can usually chuck to the wind such bothersome profit parasites as percentage rents and cost-of-living rental increments that add to the income margins of landowners. The absence of profit sharing further strengthens the value of the unit as security. If instead the purchaser had purchased a long-term leasehold, applying for a substantial leasehold mortgage, the ground rental and other charges payable to the lessor would be expected to contain profit-sharing terms that would periodically dilute the business effect of increased profitability of the particular business.

7. The condominium unit being appraised for security value should be examined for special prestige characteristics flowing from unit ownership. These sometimes may be found in the naming of a building for the purchasing firm, in the right to a valuable advertising sign overlooking

a prime audience, or in the excellence of location. Factors such as these tend to entrench a purchaser in a building for many years.

8. A business condominium's common areas may be the locale for services to unit owners not ordinarily furnished in other types of buildings. Conference rooms, display theatres, showrooms, exhibit halls, cafeterias, employee swimming pools, as well as other recreational and business conveniences may not be financially feasible for the owner of a rental building to provide to his tenants. Most individual tenants would be too limited by their leases and space requirements to build and maintain such accommodations themselves. Condominiums, by the pooling of common areas and competent space management, may often be expected to offer a larger number of such facilities to purchasers and their employees and customers. Smaller companies may thus be treated to luxurious services, such as decorous exhibition areas, that might otherwise not be available. The appraiser must focus on such factors as well.

9. Space saving, with ensuing cost efficiencies, can result from business condominiums in which there is joint use of expensive machinery and equipment, as in a medical complex containing newly invented testing instruments. Apart from the prohibitive cost to any one unit owner who might wish to purchase or rent the equipment alone, the condominium format, by common use arrangements, might save on the cost of space for separately utilizing the same equipment, thereby accruing even larger benefits. The constant fear of obsolescence of expensive equipment can be offset partially by a pooling effort for purchase or rental of such items, a method possible without relinquishing the total independence of operations by the separate owners. Existence of common areas allows cooperative business efforts without any participant's having to work in space solely owned by others. In some situations the condominium may yield a unique chance for space and cost savings not even comparable to lesser possibilities from other real estate relationships for controlling space. Factors such as these will test the appraiser's acumen.

10. Condominium units, as with other realty owned in fee simple, may appreciate or decrease in market value with the passage of time. The extent of possibilities in this direction may be difficult to project in localities in which the business condominium concept is new and an established resale market is nonexistent.

11. The appraiser of even one business unit must also seek out factors affecting the entire condominium regime, for example, the expiration dates for building services employee contracts and the trend in wage increases over past years. The quality and cost of building management concerns every unit. An erroneous or intentionally underestimated budget can mean higher costs to all owners.

Appraisals of a full building, or of a large number of units, could encompass building-wide statistics as a part of the task undertaken. But if the appraisal is for only a single unit in a multiunit complex, detailed evaluation of the total regime's information and statistics may be a burdensome task. Much depends on management's attitude of cooperation and efficient central record keeping.

12. If an existing structure is being converted to a condominium regime, caution should be exercised in reviewing property tax assessments. The typical formula of tax authorities is to divide the total assessment by unit common interest percentages to fix each separate unit assessment. Sometimes the result is inequitable and may dampen the interest of prospective future purchasers, or place immense burdens on existing owners.

Another problem caused by tax authorities is their swift tendency to reassess on the basis of the new total purchase prices of all units, rather than on the original assessment on the building when operated on a rental basis by the prior owner. Under such approach, a sizeable and sometimes shocking increase in tax assessments may loom in the future.

In renewal areas, note should be taken of government attitudes supporting abatement or lessening of tax burdens on new industry sought for the community. When legislation exists that would permit limitation on tax burdens of new businesses moving into a community, the terms and limitations of such policy should be carefully reviewed by the appraiser for both present and future effects.

13. The appraiser should not conclude his final report without reviewing a draft of the declaration and bylaws. The degree to which the board of managers may vote action affecting a unit is pertinent to the appraiser. Too often bank representatives appraise units without adequate review of underlying documents. The appraiser should prefer to rely on a brick and mortar review of property, with some analysis of economic factors, without having to plow through complex condominium documentation. This is especially true if only one or two units are the subject of an appraisal. However, the art of condominium appraisal must include a documentary review from the appraisal standpoint, even if the bank's attorneys meticulously study every word of every document. The appraiser is concerned with the highest and best use of property, and the limitations on that use that do or would affect value. In the case of a condominium, the governing documents of the regime may directly or indirectly later influence market valuation of the individual units. They must be reviewed by the appraiser.

14. The self-sufficiency of unit owners in exercising responsibility for repairs and improvements for operating premises may mean that in

later years there will be a need to refinance existing unit mortgages. A greater problem will exist if major financing will be needed for commonly used areas, because no overall mortgage will exist that can be refinanced. Any funds for such latter purposes must be forthcoming from immediate unit assessments or from reserves built up periodically to handle such problems.

The more physically separated the units, the larger the likelihood that major improvements can be refinanced by use of the separate unit mortgage. Care should be exercised if substantial heating, air conditioning or other central facilities are common elements. Reserves for repairs and improvements should take into account the eventual requirements of expensive supplanting, replacement, or overhaul of major common elements.

When the condominium is new, with adequate warranties obtained for many new facilities and important equipment, the bylaws should provide for some form of board power to collect later the reserves for future improvements. The bylaws should, nevertheless, authorize the entering of loans by the regime backed by the credit of all unit owners, subject to their consent. As a practical problem, such loans cannot be secured by units unless subject to existing prior mortgages. If the number of unit owners is small, this procedure may prove practical, but much will depend on the individual attitude of unit owners and their approach later to needed physical changes in the regime. It would seem protective to empower the board to borrow on the credit of one or more owners willing to obligate themselves to some degree when unanimity among all unit owners is impossible to obtain.

The appraiser should be especially cautious about reserves when analyzing an older property, such as one to be converted to condominium. If major improvements and rehabilitation must be effected, it may be essential that this all be done by the sponsor just prior to conveyance of unit title to purchasers. In this fashion, the institutional lender can be assured that the condominium starts life in excellent condition, without the immediate tactical problem of assessing heavy charges against purchasers.

An appraiser looking at an older building in this context, must inquire about the mechanical means for raising funds for improvements. With the passage of time, and more experience with the subject, new devices for bank protection will doubtlessly be found.

UNIT OWNERS WHO LEASE TO OTHERS: LEASEHOLD MORTGAGES

Let us assume that the owner of one of ten condominium units in a medical building wishes to issue a 15-year lease to a partnership of three eminent surgeons. To enter the lease, the unit owner wishes 150,000 dollars in cash from the prospective lessees, who are willing to enter into a leasehold mortgage to secure the major portion of this sum. It is doubtful that any bank would grant such a loan without some form of subordination of key documents, including the lease, mortgages on the unit, and probably the condominium declaration. The bank would need some guarantee of nondisturbance of the lease as security if there is a default by the lessee on the lease, or if the unit owner reneges on his own mortgage or on condominium obligations for maintenance charges or otherwise. In ordinary leasehold mortgage transactions, it is customary for banks to be assured that they themselves will be able to cure any defaults that may lead to defeasance of lease security, and to be given adequate notice of lease imperilment. In the case of condominium unit leases, it may be expected that similar demands be made. However, if the declaration and unit mortgages do not allow for such a procedure in their original form, it will probably not be possible to obtain leasehold mortgages in transactions of the type described above. Later amendment of those documents will be difficult because of mortgagee intransigence and the rarity of the near-unanimous consent required of other unit owners. In planning a new condominium, or in refinancing for condominium conversions, it is essential that this type of future leasehold financing opportunity be considered, to increase the value of units for passive investors seeking long-term lessees.

A related problem involves the substitution by the lending institution of new lessees. Ordinarily, a business condominium would in some way restrict in bylaws the selection of long-term occupants other than assignees of unit owners. If the right of approval in the board must be met by banks seeking new lessees on a default, the value of their investment might be considerably jeopardized. For this reason institutional lenders should consider requiring bylaw provisions waiving such rights, or at least leaving its exercise to the discretion of a reputable managing agent. This procedure would be consistent with customary waiver by condominium regimes, by bylaw or declaration provision, of the right of first refusal on foreclosure of first mortgage liens on defaulting unit owners.

CONSTRUCTION LOANS

The construction lender who is offered business condominium developments is posed with unique problems. Most troublesome would be estimating the likelihood of acceptability of this new form of ownership, not only by purchasers but by permanent lenders who are needed to take out the construction loans, replacing them with permanent financing.

It may be expected that construction lenders will be more insistent than with other loans in requiring permanent loan "take outs," which in this case would mean coverage for most or all of the condominium units to be created.

Permanent lenders may not readily wish to commit themselves in advance of construction without a substantial degree of preselling by the developer that assures the purchase of space by good security risks. Certain marketplace factors must be overcome before permanent mortgage lenders, in many instances, decide to issue loans. These factors relate to attitudes of business firms that are offered units to be constructed. Chief among these are the following:

1. Many firms do not want to commit themselves until they can physically see the new buildings going up, for fear of the physical appearance of the new condominium structure.

2. Many business firms might fear committing themselves to new construction until they know the other participants who will share in condominium ownership.

3. Some firms hesitate because the newness of condominium construction does not permit an examination of past real estate experience as a guide to predicting resale value of units to be purchased.

4. Many firms ordinarily do not like to commit themselves a long time in advance, if construction of a large structure will take a substantial period of time.

The aforesaid problems facing the permanent lender will, of necessity, also confront the construction lender seeking commitments for permanent loans as insurance against repayment of funds advanced. However, one important factor absent in residential housing does somewhat lessen these problems. In residential housing construction, many of the condominiums are built in areas that would not permit a rental alternative because of zoning laws. On the other hand, most commercial space is constructed in areas in which zoning permits the alternative of ownership or leasing without too much difficulty. Thus if a building has good potential for use on a rental basis, the security for the loan would seem to be substantially protected even if there is difficulty in preselling condominium units or in obtaining permanent loan commitments.

The issuance of permanent loan commitments without preselling presents another special problem to the construction lender. Ordinarily, a builder can obtain a construction loan more easily on rental property in which a permanent lender issues a commitment to take out the construction loan. Because the party mortgagor in both cases is the same person or entity, the transaction is relatively simple. However, even if permanent loans are committed in case of the building condominium for all the units, the absence of preselling still jeopardizes the finality of the transaction because of the unknown factor of attractiveness to purchasers. Therefore, the conservative approach by construction lenders will probably require preselling as well as permanent loan commitments. In certain cases in which the preselling has involved outstanding credit risks or well-established firms with substantial cash positions, permanent loan commitments may not be as important.

As has been the case in several instances to date, construction lenders interested in building a business condominium have conditioned lending on the developer's meeting of standards applicable to rental buildings, so that the security for the loan will be fully protected in traditional ways. This procedure actually has made the lending process somewhat simpler for developers because of acceptable attitudes and practices in rental construction in many cases. For example, office and professional buildings are sometimes built without major tenants, or with a minimum of presigned leases. Commercial space has been created in this fashion in many areas of the country, often with considerable success when renting begins. The stumbling block in the condominium process, where interspersed as the key alternative in that procedure, would be the nature of the space created. Purchasing unit owners may be more demanding of the form in which their space is created, perhaps quite differently from the ordinary tenant. For this reason it is much more preferable for building plans to be devoted to known, specific tenants to whom the units have been presold.

The construction lender unsatisfied with preselling and take-out commitments may wish to place limitations on the freedom of the developer to finalize contracts with purchasers. With this device the construction lender can prevent a small number of sales of units turning the building into a condominium with substantially vacant space that jeopardizes the security of the loan. In that connection, the construction lender may want to place conditions on the number of sales of units and the quality of the purchasers before permitting the builder's contractual obligations to deliver to be final, which would forestall conversion of the building to rental use.

Because the success of the construction loan is so tied to final success of the condominium, it is likely that many construction lenders will also seriously consider the issuing of permanent mortgages on finalized units.

Another construction problem must be faced—the complexity of security tied to undivided interests once units are separately released from the overall construction loan, a procedure required by many state laws and permanent lenders. Most commercial condominiums to date have been high- or low-rise single buildings in which unit occupancy is not possible until total completion of the entire group of units. Once a construction lender releases any unit from the blanket loan, the security backing the remainder of the loan is composed of finished units and applicable undivided interests in common areas, items having substantial security value. If remaining units cannot be sold, the lending institution has valuable space available for renting to offset unpaid sums under its loan.

However, in the case of horizontal construction, the problem is more difficult. If one of twelve attached or detached units is constructed and conveyed on release of the construction loan, the remaining security to the construction lender is obstructed by the undivided interest in common areas that has been conveyed to the initial purchaser. In effect, the construction loan becomes subordinated to the declaration. Because this problem also exists with residential housing, construction lender demands for preselling have been high, usually 50 percent or more, in residential developments of this type. Such demands are likely to be carried over to business condominiums as well.

When residential condominium construction began after 1960 in the United States, there was substantial hesitation by lending institutions concerning the security value of the product being created through use of institutional financing. The passage of time has resulted in the acceleration of that form of housing to a point where it may become the most important type of residential housing constructed in the years to come. It is the author's belief that business condominiums may present a similar situation in which a slow beginning will suddenly accelerate. To achieve this acceleration the construction lender must play an exceedingly important role.

THE PERMANENT UNIT MORTGAGEE

We have already discussed some of the problems facing the permanent lender when asked for mortgage commitments before construction loans are obtained from other institutions. Let us review some other aspects of lending practices specially important in business condominium unit permanent financing. These can be placed in the following categories:

1. Adequate flexibility on foreclosure.
2. Protection against expandable condominium regimes.
3. Reserves for repairs and improvements to common elements.

4. Specialized or general business utilization of space.
5. Relations with secondary mortgagees.
6. Mortgage restrictions against mortgagor voting and other acts.
7. Escrow arrangements to protect security.

ADEQUATE FLEXIBILITY ON FORECLOSURE

Two problems are the concern of the permanent unit mortgagee when there is a default by the borrower. The value of the unit in the marketplace at such time would probably be the foremost consideration. Much will depend on the accuracy of the original economic appraisal of unit values. Secondly, the mechanical formula to liquidate security must be realistic and unhampered by bylaw restrictions. Technical aspects of condominium ownership must be initially understood by the prospective mortgagee to assure basic protection for liquidation techniques.

The lender should guard against future imposition of unreasonable bylaw restrictions on resales by mortgagees on unit owner defaults. Thus such ordinary curbs as the right of first refusal by the board on new purchasers might have to be altered to protect the institutional lender. The mortgages of unit owners would otherwise, of necessity, be subject to the terms and conditions of the declaration and bylaws as they relate to decisions or actions taken by persons other than the contracting mortgagor.

Another practical problem to be faced at foreclosure time, relating to liquidation of security, is the availability of permission to make major alterations or improvements within the particular unit involved in a mortgage default. Saleability often depends on the right of a new owner to redivide by removing or adding partitions; emplacement of new forms of machinery, equipment, or personnel; and other changes required by a new business owner. The tremendous variations in business operations by different companies must be contemplated when considering sales on foreclosure. Condominium governing documents should be studied for restrictive powers or limitations that would inhibit freedom of disposition on foreclosure.

A lending institution approached for permanent loan commitments by a sponsor should review drafts of declaration and bylaw documents. At this early moment, before construction or conveyance of unit titles, a prospective mortgagee can exercise enormous influence in placing conditions and limitations in these documents for both immediate and future protection. Sometimes the documents contain clauses applicable to lenders of "25 percent or more of total units," "two or more units," or even "one or more units."

If a sponsor begins construction without having obtained long-term mortgage commitments for unit purchase mortgages, he should nevertheless insert protective clauses in his documents that would be expected to be required at a later time by lending institutions contemplating issuing mortgages.

PROTECTION AGAINST EXPANDABLE OR CONSTRICTABLE CONDOMINIUM REGIMES

It has become increasingly customary in recent years for developers of all forms of condominiums to provide for expansion of condominium regimes or tie-ups with other developments planned for the future by the same builder or his controlled entities. A widening of the development and an increase in units have posed problems for lenders in residential promotions; these techniques also pose difficulties for lenders in commercial ventures. Some commercial condominiums, especially shopping centers, have given such latitude for change to developers that the clauses in the condominium documents expressly provide that the expansion provisions are severable if they are determined to be contrary to the state condominium act.

A lender reviewing a loan program ordinarily must evaluate the effects of success or failure of a builder's overall program, because of the potential influence of total composition on the market value of any part of the realty underwritten. Unlike traditional real estate, the commercial condominium rests on relationships with property owned by others through use of commonly owned facilities. If, by expansion of the regime, increased numbers of unit owners must use such facilities, it is possible that the value of individual units may be decreased. If sales turn out to be less than contemplated, it is possible that the changes burdening individual owners for common facilities may be excessive, thereby adding a diminishing factor to the value of each unit as security for the loan.

Broadening a condominium regime, by adding more units than originally contemplated, may also add new institutional lenders to the venture, bringing new bank competition and increasing the voices asserting rights of decision making or vetoes given lending institutions in governing condominium documents. A prestigious group of original owners may find marginal firms added to the list of owners, thereby lessening the value of units as security.

Vague rights to expand a regime, granted or reserved by the developer, present an important factor for the lending institution trying to evaluate the worthiness of particular security. In a commerical condominium regime, a great deal of convenience and value to the unit owner may be lost by unbridled rights of the developer to keep building and adding new units, or to create contractual obligations between two or more regimes.

It would often seem reasonable, from the bank's point of view, to condition the terms and conditions of the declaration and bylaws covering the construction or addition of new units, or covering relationships with other regimes that involve some dilution of ownership rights, including convenience and the right of first refusal of new entrants.

RESERVES FOR REPAIRS AND IMPROVEMENTS TO COMMON ELEMENTS

Permanent lenders should insist that the original bylaws empower the board of managers to assess owners for current charges and reserves to be used to replace or improve the common elements. On occasion it may seem reasonable to require a minimum percentage of common charges to be placed regularly in a reserve pool. The reason for this approach should be apparent, considering that there is no overall mortgage blanketing all units that can be refinanced or recast to raise the requisite funds immediately for such purposes. Each condominium unit mortgage stands alone, and ordinarily it can be used only to finance self-contained and divisible improvements that can constitute mortgage security.

However, if a passage of time does lead to a substantial increase in the value of individual unit mortgage security, some relief from this predicament might be forthcoming. If a substantial board assessment is made on each unit for an immediately required, expensive, common improvement such as a new heating system, permanent lenders might refinance separate unit mortgages to provide the amount of assessment, thereby reflecting the increased market value of the unit and undivided interest, conditioned as well by the increase in value coming from the improvement to the common elements. This sort of attitude by lenders will have to emerge in years to come as a matter of self-preservation of their security.

SPECIALIZED OR GENERAL BUSINESS UTILIZATION OF SPACE

Many future business condominium complexes will be made up, as some are already, of firms engaged in the same profession or business. The most obvious examples are medical professional buildings and specialized industry structures such as a commercial printing industry building.

Throughout the gamut of commercial enterprise one saving grace for many individuals and businesses unable to succeed has been the inflationary price movement of space owned. With the use of market appreciation of existing property, debts have been paid and even a profit sometimes gained when ordinary business operations just did not prove justifiable. To the mortgagee, the likelihood of good resale possibilities is important, but not only for foreclosure purposes. Just as pertinent is the likelihood of security resale value that will assure debt payments and discharge. Moreover, the potential of turnover from good resale markets also contributes the good possibility of new lending opportunities for the lender, tailored to the then-current interest and amortization rates.

The more specialized a regime and its participants, however, the less flexibility in resale opportunities. That is not to say that in individual cases the resale opportunities will not be greater in some areas for specialized properties in great demand.

Commercial condominium properties often contain intertwining relationships among firms required to share common facilities. It is sometimes apparent that the balance of operations sensitively depends on such connections. In other instances, the efficiency and business aid occasioned by cooperative use of facilities is of less basic importance. The prospective lending institution should review the incidence and results of interdependency and cooperation to determine whether the regime has been tailored to specific companies, with difficulties to ensue if unit owners sell or assign their interests to others; or, more happily for the lender, whether the opportunities flowing from condominium ownership could create considerable interest from other businesses seeking to purchase the units of original purchasers.

RELATIONS WITH SECONDARY MORTGAGEES

Business owners of real estate make wider use of second mortgage financing than residential unit owners. The principal reason is that usually the acquisition of business property requires a smaller percentage of cost made up of mortgage funds, whereas residential units sometimes are financed up to 95 percent of cost. Business realty financing is considered substantial if it reaches the 75 or 80 percent level. In many instances the first mortgage lending on commercial properties does not exceed 50 percent of appraised value, especially for older properties.

The purchaser of business real estate must often, because of the aforesaid conditions, look for second mortgage financing to reduce the necessary cash outlay when purchasing particular property. Customarily, issuers of first mortgages on business property allow their security to be further subject to second liens. Sometimes the second mortgagee must have the approval of the institution holding the first mortgage; at other times, there is no mention of the subject in the original mortgage.

Thus far, many business condominium regimes have been financed by unit first mortgagees that appear to be substantially higher than typically available for business real estate ventures. One reason may be the difficulty in obtaining second mortgage money in a field as new as the business condominium. One consideration may be that the degree of "flipping" or assignment of second mortgage notes ordinarily is much greater than first business liens, especially if the secondary funds come from noninstitutional sources; subsequent purchasers of second liens may be wary of new forms of ownership. Moreover, many business condominiums involve new construction, in which borrowings tend to be higher.

The protections against incursions on first lien security by second mortgages would be similar to those required for ordinary business property. In some states, statutory safeguards or court decisions make such protection ample without denotation in the mortgage instruments. In other states, a list of do's and don'ts for mortgagors is listed in the first mortgage instrument as applicable to subsequent mortgages covering the property.

Some of the additional protection required by first mortgagees as against second lien holders might be:

1. The right to pass on the selection of second mortgagees. In some instances the emphasis may be on institutional lenders rather than speculators.

2. The right to pass on the contents of the second mortgage documents to assure noninterference with the terms of the first mortgage, as well as compliance with the terms and purposes of the declaration and bylaws of the condominium regime.

MORTGAGE RESTRICTIONS AGAINST MORTGAGOR VOTING AND OTHER ACTS

We have already evaluated possible provisions in the declaration and bylaws aimed at protecting mortgagees investing loans in business condominium units. Such clauses should be coordinated with the terms and conditions of each individual permanent mortgage to assure workable implementation of both. For example, a permanent mortgage may include a clause providing for the right of foreclosure whenever the board of managers does not maintain adequate hazard and liability policies. The mortgage clauses requiring each unit owner to pay his share of these charges thus would have added implicitly the obligation to vote and otherwise pursue unit owner rights to influence the board to utilize payments appropriately for such purposes. With this technique the terms of the declaration requiring adequate insurance are merged with individual responsibilities placed on unit owners in their separate mortgages.

As an alternative to foreclosure, some lenders also seek the right standby to perform some or all of the covenants and obligations of unit owners under the declaration and bylaws, even though liens by boards would ordinarily be subservient to first mortgages. One reason for this attitude would be the desire to assure that the board collects adequate insurance proceeds, thereby avoiding the jeopardization of all condominium units. This subject should be covered in the bylaws as well as in individual unit mortgages.

A review of business condominium mortgage documents indicates different approaches, or even silence, with respect to restrictions on the unit owner's right to vote and otherwise act on various topics in which the mortgagee might wish to maintain lingering control. Unit mortgage clauses might be considered that give the mortgagee the right of foreclosure if the mortgagor engages, without the permission of the lender, in any of the following:

1. Votes to amend the declaration or bylaws.
2. Votes to terminate the regime because of physical damage.
3. Votes for a withdrawal of the regime from condominium status for any other reason.
4. Votes to end the use of an independent managing agent.
5. Refuses to furnish the lender with copies of notices or documents pertaining to the condominium (usually applicable to votes at meetings).
6. Does not pay assessments and common charges nor otherwise comply with the declaration and bylaws of the regime.
7. Changes or abandons the chief occupation or profession originally represented to be the purpose for securing the mortgage loan.
8. Leases the premises to others.
9. Sells or assigns the business or premises to others.

In some situations adequate notice to lenders may be enough, with consent presumed after passage of a reasonable time. Otherwise, actual affirmative consent may be required.

Limitations on unit owners, such as those enumerated above, are important considerations to lenders who are approached to finance resales, as well as on original commitments. In addition, the terms of other mortgages on units, not the subject of mortgage applications, should also be evaluated. If firms already in the regime must abide by rules of other mortgagees that tend to assure the structure's permanent, efficient direction, as in the case of a needed professional medical building, the new mortgagee can better judge the nature and scope of the security backing a condominium unit loan in the same development.

Even with such restrictions in mortgage documents, the most important documents to the lender still must be the declaration and bylaws. Decisive majority votes could eventuate without the acquiescence of any particular mortgagor. Yet the right to foreclose may be too impractical and fearsome a remedy in all cases. Much more preferable are workable declaration and bylaw requirements that such key matters as amendments to declarations and bylaws on certain categories of subjects be conditioned on the consent of all mortgagees holding a substantial percentage of loans, such as 10 or 25 percent. If a regime contains very few units, unanimity among mortgagees may be essential.

Although undue interference with condominium business should not be authorized or attempted by mortgagees, the nature of condominium ownership forces the lender to reach beyond his mortgage instrument for authority over the acts of persons other than his own mortgagor. For such right, the master documents must spell out authorization, and clearly. One of the weakest features of many documents in use in Puerto Rico and South America for business regimes has been inattention to lender rights beyond the strictures of individual mortgages. American attempts at commercial unit mortgages have usually been fashioned on residential precedents, rather than foreign documents. Fortunately, a few items were properly copied. Unfortunately, the special significance of a business enterprise has often been overlooked. More experience by institutions should help solve this problem. Foreign precedents for document drafting appear to be of limited value.

ESCROW ARRANGEMENTS TO PROTECT SECURITY

Whatever a bank or insurance company outlook on escrowing property taxes and other charges in other business mortgagee situations, there would seem no substantial reasons to alter such policy merely because condominium business units are involved.

Unlike the widespread uniformity apparent in lender approach to escrow accounts for homeowner residential housing, commercial loans tend to be more subjective and changeable as among borrowers. This latter approach means that a lending institution may wish to establish escrow accounts for various items for different borrowers, even within the same regime.

Large commercial rental developments often hire experienced, bonded management that must first collect general rents before placing them in ordinary or special accounts for expense items, including taxes and mortgage obligations. Delays in payments may mean poor management as often as a lack of funds. In the case of the condominium, the mortgage indebtedness is payable directly by each owner, meaning that defaults in payment of such funds would be readily apparent to the lender. As for other charges, such as insurance of condominium common areas and overall hazard policies, these payments must be made on a timely basis to the board of managers, or its appointed managing agent. Defaults would be quickly apparent; in such instances the banks may be benefitted by bylaw provisions requiring or permitting notification of respective lenders of their mortgagor's defaults.

In view of the lower percentage-to-value ratio of commercial loans compared with homeowner mortgages, there is likely to be less of the frenetic concern for loss of security value in the commercial venture that has led to stringent escrow requirements for homeowners. Nevertheless, each investment by institutions must be carefully evaluated for special factors that may necessitate some degree of safeguarding procedure in the business condominium. Lenders do try to avoid needless and expensive bookkeeping that serves little purpose. In the case of the condominium, a great deal can be accomplished by requiring the mortgagor and the regime to give timely notice to lenders of conditions or states of fact that are of urgent importance in safeguarding security values.

FRONT-END SYNDICATION BY PURCHASERS

A developer of a new business condominium, or one involving substantial revamping of an existing building, can benefit from the new condominium concept in a special way. It is quite likely that down payments by participation unit owners can be amassed, assuming a successful selling campaign, that would exceed nonlender sources for initiating funds in other types of ventures. That is to say, the construction of a mere rental building would not involve initial payments for security deposits and related matters that would come close to the larger initial payments required for purchasers of units in a condominium. Also, it is quite likely that the total of all business unit purchases or deposits before construction or rehabilitation will be considerably higher than the single typical down payment made by a firm that will become a net lessee of a building being created for that purpose.

Front-end money that is available without interest costs can considerably enhance the viability of a venture needing substantial amounts of capital. In most cases commercial mortgage loans for development and construction will still be essential, but any reduction in the amounts needed will be a valuable incentive to proceed via the condominium route. The formulas employed by banks and other lenders in construction lending involve actual money costs far in excess of permanent loans, as well as stage payment procedures that continually limit the availability of funds. In addition, it is often possible to obtain more favorable lending terms when the amount of the loan is reduced as against total construction requirements.

In effect, the purchasers of such business condominiums are themselves syndicators who have pooled together initial deposits to enable the process of construction to be initiated and to proceed expeditiously, even though under legal concepts they may not be considered the promoters of the venture at this early moment.

One of the most difficult problems in developing new and imaginative real estate concepts to fruition is the difficulty in obtaining front money that aids in initiating a development. For this reason, the business condominium concept, where successful, may be of considerable aid in easing the process.

CLASSIFICATIONS OF INVESTOR SYNDICATIONS

Pools of investors acting together as a group to achieve investment income from business condominiums can be divided into three categories.

The promoter-developer may be a real estate syndication in which a number of persons participate, either as stockholders of a corporation or as limited partners in a promoting partnership. The preferred form is usually the limited partnership, even though intermediary construction corporations may be established by a partnership during some stages of development. If the corporation is used, it is oftentimes in subchapter S form whereby investors achieve a conduit type of tax treatment that eliminates double taxation at the corporate level, thereby achieving some of the benefits of a partnership. Creators of business condominiums who obviously build them for resale face ordinary income tax rates on profits from the sale of units, although the circumstances and term of control relating to land ownership will govern the availability of capital gains type treatment with respect to the sale of land.

Another form of syndication possible is that of groups of developers who have entered a pooling arrangement with lenders whereby mortgagees share somewhat in profit potential from sales of units.

A more lingering category of syndication in business condominiums is made up of groups of investors who seek to invest in completed units for rental income purposes and eventual resale opportunities. Fine opportunities for creative investments may become available. For example, three union pension funds may together invest in a condominium complex that encompasses three business firms offering large numbers of jobs to members of the respective unions.

SYNDICATE INVESTING IN PERMANENT UNITS

We may expect in the future that business condominium promoters will seek to establish or attract limited partnerships investing in completed business condominium units, or other investors seeking rental income. Such promotions will probably be of two types. In one case, each partner will be offered a limited partnership interest in one unit or a group of condominium units rather than the sole and exclusive single ownership of any particular unit. For group syndicate ownership the importance of management availability is obvious, necessitating strong reliance by passive investors on the capability of good management. The tax law and regulations relating to limited partnerships have now been defined to an extent to which careful arrangements by expert counsel can probably obtain conduit tax treatment for investors who may benefit from real estate tax shelters occasioned by depreciation allowances. Another type of promotion we may soon see would involve arrangements whereby each investor obtains exclusive ownership of a particular unit which he may rent to others. Here the problem of management is somewhat more complex, because some purchasers may wish to manage units themselves, whereas others may wish to take a passive approach. The promoting developer would have to consider the types of management available and controls necessary to attract investors and promote harmonious operation of the entire condominium regime.

It is quite possible that a large industrial condominium complex might end up with central management directed by the board of managers, with different industrial plants and offices individually managed by others on behalf of operating firms or outside investors, as the case may be. Much depends on the physical nature of the condominium regime and the type of purchasers of units attracted by the developer.

SECURITIES LAW PROBLEMS

It should be remembered that the offering of real estate syndication interests, such as limited partnership participations, may constitute a course of conduct requiring registration under federal and state securities laws. The mere sale of business condominium units would not seem to involve the type of investment contract calling for security treatment. In S.E.C. Release No. 5347, issued on January 4, 1973, on condominium registration it was stated:

"In summary, the offering of condominium units in conjunction with any one of the following will cause the offering to be viewed as an offering of securities in the form of investment contracts:

1. The condominiums, with any rental arrangement or other similar service, are offered and sold with emphasis on the economic benefits to the purchaser to be derived from the managerial efforts of the promoter, or a third party designated or arranged for by the promoter, from rental of the units.

2. The offering of participation in a rental pool arrangement; and

3. The offering of a rental or similar arrangement whereby the purchaser must hold his unit available for rental for any part of the year, must use an exclusive rental agent or is otherwise materially restricted in his occupancy or rental of his unit."

In all of the foregoing situations, investor protection requires the application of the federal securities laws.

"If the condominiums are not offered and sold with emphasis on the economic benefits to the purchaser to be derived from the managerial efforts of others, and assuming that no plan to avoid the registration requirements of the Securities Act is involved, an owner of a condominium unit may, after purchasing his unit, enter into a non-pooled rental arrangement with an agent not designated or required to be used as a condition to the purchase, whether or not such agent is affiliated with the offeror, without causing a sale of a security to be involved in the sale of the unit. Further a continuing affiliation between the developers or promoters of a project and the project by reason of maintenance arrangements does not make the unit a security.

"In situations where commercial facilities are a part of the common elements of a residential project, no registration would be required under the investment contract theory where (a) the income from such facilities is used only to offset common area expenses and (b) the operation of such facilities is incidental to the project as a whole and are not established as a primary income source for the individual owners of a condominium or cooperative unit."

Although this release was issued primarily in connection with the growing number of resort development rental pools, the language would appear to have considerable significance for commercial condominiums as well, and should be reviewed in that connection.

A sharp distinction lies between the sale of units to entrepreneurs and the sale of syndication shares to investors who will generally participate passively in ownership of groups of units, utilizing the promoter or others for supervision and management on their behalf, that is, establishing a managed rental pool for their benefit. If investors such as limited partners rely on administration and control by others, own assignable interests, and would be considered as members of the investing public (rather than a confined private group), it is quite likely that securities registration problems may ensue. Whether statutory private offering exemptions apply will depend on individual circumstances and the then-existing federal and state law. The so-called "intrastate" offering exemption for sales made within a single state has been drastically narrowed by courts and the Securities and Exchange Commission in recent years. Moreover, many states now provide formidable regulation in this area.

We may expect development of imaginative devices to encourage the flow of investment funds, once the business condominium reaches popularity. Each such method must be examined for securities law aspects, as well as against ordinary condominium legal procedures.

Once an offering comes within the scope of securities statutes, one must expect that at the least a full disclosure of all material details will have to be made to the offerees. This procedure protects the developer as well as the offeree, avoiding spurious charges of misrepresentation. In addition, in many states securities administrators are empowered to pass on the "fair, just, and equitable" quality of securities offerings. Such latter powers have in the past led to restrictions on the terms of management agreements, the amount of promoter profits, and other key matters. Once an offering is defined as involving securities, whether or not formal registration is required, the strictures of civil antifraud penalties hover over the promoter, as in the case of Rule 10-b(5) of the federal securities law. In this area the developer has great need for competent legal counsel experienced in securities regulatory matters.

In New York State, all offerings of condominiums, irrespective of the residential or nonresidential use indicated, are subject to regulation by the state attorney general. However, a special regulation exists under which an offering may be accepted in that state from commercial developers without the otherwise required summary prospectus. The section of the applicable regulations states:

"Notwithstanding any other provision of this Part, in the case of a wholly nonresidential condominium project or development offering, the filing and delivery of an offering plan consisting of true copies of the declaration and bylaws may be accepted by the Attorney-General as adequate."

One of the reasons for this special rule in New York is the difficulty in summarizing the detailed business and financial activities of each commercial participant when the offering is first begun. However, in most cases New York requires a total set of offering documents that thoroughly details sufficient information for commercial offerees and their attorneys. It is assumed by the regulators of this state that individual business enterprises will retain attorneys who will thoroughly research the particular venture involved and the identification and quality of the other participants. It is considered good practice for developers in New York to supply prospective purchasers with details on all prior purchasers who have contracted to buy, to give the full benefits of disclosure. Under present practice in New York, the attorney general usually accepts the declaration and bylaws as adequate offering literature if very few units are involved. However, if the offering is extensive, a formal offering brochure, tailored to the commercial undertaking, is generally required. In most instances a developer himself needs such offering literature to sell.

In most other states, if a securities offering (syndication) solely involves direct sale of *investment* units in a business condominium development, jurisdiction would appear to be in the hands of the state securities commissioner, who often has extensive powers to regulate securities offerings. Reliance by investors on promoter management of units, pooling of income, and similar securities aspects may point the venture to such characterization.

SOME REFLECTIONS ON FINANCING

In this chapter we have attempted to evaluate various kinds of financing techniques applicable to business condominiums. It should be apparent that the tools for the accomplishment of a condominium development lean heavily on an affirmative attitude by institutional lenders and others who provide financing of business in the American economy. A great deal of study and reflection will be necessary by these sources of funds before they are thoroughly convinced that the field of business condominiums poses substantial opportunities for profit making and new contributions to American business development. It is the author's belief that a large number of affirmative factors, as detailed throughout this book, provide substantial impetus for lenders who wish to enter this field.

LEASEHOLD BUSINESS CONDOMINIUMS

In the case of leasehold condominiums, the underlying land involved in the venture will not be owned by the unit owners, unlike the fee simple type of condominium organization; each unit owner will only obtain a lease arrangement between himself and the owner of the land. In some cases the lease will be a participation sublease in an overall leasing of land by the owner to the condominium regime or an intermediary primary lessee. In most cases leasehold condominium developments have involved the fragmentation of the land ownership so that individual separate unit leases are entered into between each unit owner and the owner of the land. With the latter device the danger of defeasance of any single unit owner's lease position is eliminated when other unit lessees default in payment of the ground rent or other obligations under their individual leases.

The declaration filed usually states the exclusive right to unit use by each lessee of defined space, with a concomitant undivided interest in the use and enjoyment of commonly utilized areas. However, unlike fee condominiums, the physically undivided right to use the land comes from a lease instrument rather than a conveyance of fee title.

Institutional lenders should be wary of leasehold condominium arrangements that do not provide a shield to individual unit owners from lease defeasance caused by the acts of others. The primary security for any mortgage given to individual unit owners will be the lease, thereby making such loans leasehold mortgages.

Under most applicable state laws, condominium unit lease mortgages can be separately given to each unit owner, in addition to the separate tax assessment that taxing authorities would set, thereby giving a substantial degree of independence to each unit owner.

Leasehold security may later be imperiled by ground lease arrangements that provide for incremental rent based on later reevaluation of land value, or for payments by unit lessees of percentages of income from the business involved in the unit lease.

The latter possibilities for landlord participation in income may nullify, in some cases, much of the real differences between condominium ownership and a landlord-tenant relationship. In cases in which government authorities own the underlying land with no participation in business income, to that degree the landlord-tenant participation problem is alleviated.

There are at least four other possible benefits of leasehold condominiums over mere renting. There is likely to be greater freedom of operations than under ordinary rental situations. Second, the terms of condominium regimes will usually be longer than many rentals, with less fearfulness of sudden demands for removal and relocation. In some cases, the possibilities for ground rental increases may be far more limited than for ordinary expectable rent increases to regular tenants. Third, the leasehold condominium may present greater opportunities for obtaining leasehold secured mortgages. Moreover, the condominium unit lessee has a vote in the management of the regime, and a veto on major decisions requiring unanimity.

All of these factors are important to the lending institution. Some developers have tried to use documentation to give the aura of fee ownership to leasehold arrangements, but the lender should be cognizant that the distinction is clear. In some states, besides unit leases, documents are given to unit holders using language such as "deed of assignment" or "deed of space." However, the lease arrangement is not fee simple ownership, because of the chance of distant reversion of the entire premises to the landowner. In some states, perpetually renewable leases may be available; in others, the designation of air space ownership includes the right to destroy any improvements before termination of the lease.

In addition, in evaluating the leasehold condominium application, the lending institution might concern itself with the following, among other matters:

1. The term of the lease and renewal features are relevant. There should be adequate time for the loan to mature prior to the end of a key leasing period.

2. The underlying ground lease should be limited by a nondisturbance clause therein that permits the leasehold mortgagee itself to cure defaults on the receipt of reasonable notice.

3. The lender should review condemnation provisions applicable to the unit, the regime, and the ground lessee to assure adequate protection of its financial position in case of a government takeover.

4. Insurance policies covering hazard and liability occurrences should be carefully reviewed on all levels to assure lender protection.

5. The lender should require substantial freedom on foreclosure to operate, resell, or sublet the condominium leasehold unit. If the loan is to continue to a sublessee, the right of *attornment* (taking the position of lessee), should be provided.

6. Title policies covering the mortgage should embrace damage claims resulting from invalidity of the condominium regime under state law, in addition to failure of land title.

In some situations, the elimination of land purchase cost may enable attractive pricing of leasehold units. In other cases, the lender's appraiser may find that pricing is too close to what fee simple ownership could have provided.

CHAPTER VII

SPECIALIZED BUSINESS CONDOMINIUM REGIMES

MEDICAL, DENTAL AND SCIENCE BUILDINGS

CHANGES IN MEDICAL PRACTICE

The past 25 years have witnessed four important changes in medical practice that have led to the new popularity of centralized professional buildings, a type of building that recently has been developed in condominium form throughout many parts of the United States. Many, if not most, doctors today rarely make house calls, thereby removing the need for neighborhood proximity to patients; swift, modern highways have eased travel for those doctors who regularly or occasionally make house calls. At the same time, the medical profession has splintered into many specialties, often posing the need for several doctors in lieu of the single practitioner who satisfied our grandparents with his amazing breadth of expertise. Third, science practitioners need more space than previously to house large units of advanced equipment and many more kinds of smaller machinery and materials. Moreover, most patients drive or are driven to doctors' offices, substantially raising the requirements for parking space.

Prior to World War II, professional medical buildings were few in number, often not exceeding the typical one-story structure that depended on a limited neighborhood clientele. Investors in the few larger structures suffered considerably during the Depression, in most cases, by rental rates that often fell to one-third or lower, although higher rentals began to emerge with the outbreak of war. It was the return of large numbers of doctors from military service at the end of World War II and the shortage of commercial space that brought an increasing demand for well-located professional buildings concentrating general and specialized aspects of medical practice.

In most instances, professional real estate developers constructed and rented out the new professional buildings. Leases tended to be short-term, to enable higher rentals once the young veterans and other lessees established lucrative practices or strengthened an initial clientele. Commercial banks issued a large number of loans to doctors that helped procure furnishings, equipment, and sometimes the clientele of patients of retiring practitioners.

Because of an urge for independence and freedom from landlord control, some doctors banded together in joint ventures by partnerships or corporations by which they financed, constructed, and occupied professional buildings themselves, often leaving several units unsubscribed and aimed at bringing in rents that would effectively lessen their own costs of operation and even give surplus income. Sometimes this was done by forming a stock cooperative. In most situations, a group of agreements were entered into among the participating venturers that guaranteed each his space requirements, and that, hopefully, shielded him from unreasonable acts by his associates. Many of these agreements tended to be vague, unresponsive to the long-term needs of the doctors, and not conducive to settlement of mutually important problems that might arise in the future.

RESPONSIBILITIES UNDER PAST PRACTICES

Before the advent of the American condominium in the 1960s, in partnership or cooperative corporation the dangers of personal losses were broad for doctors associating themselves with such noncondominium ventures for the purpose of securing personal office space, in addition to any income investment that motivated the move.

An ordinary general or limited partnership of doctors financing a professional medical building would be expected to fund the promotion by a single underlying mortgage or group of mortgages secured by the entire property. If the partnership is entirely *general*, then each partner is usually singly and severally liable for all mortgage and other debts as well as the liabilities of other types incurred by the partnership. If some of the partners are *limited,* they may have effectively shielded themselves from general personal liability if all statutory state requirements for filing are met. Nevertheless, a default in payment of the entire mortgage could lead to a foreclosure, wiping out the individual limited partner's interest.

If a corporation were established instead, purportedly a cooperative or not, then mere individual stockholders might be protected from general individual liability for corporate debts and obligations, but, again, the value of their stockholding investment could vanish if the entire building mortgage were not paid and foreclosure followed.

What has been said about mortgages applies similarly to real property taxes assessed against the partnership or corporate owner of the entire land and realty improvements encompassing the undertaking. Default in payment of the entire amount levied could lead to a disastrous tax foreclosure, even if any individual doctor has himself regularly paid his share of all amounts he agreed to contribute. The only alternative would be higher payments to make up for deficiencies from defaulting associates.

In many cases, by necessity, such partnership and corporate participation was conditioned by underlying agreements and contractual arrangements governing the building's operation and administration, as well as the rights of the partaking doctors as among themselves. In effect, most such ventures required agreement for cooperative enterprise, especially on commonly used facilities and areas. Accompanying such procedure, however, was the lurking danger of loss of investment if other venturers could not or would not pay their share of total mortgage or real property taxes. In an actual 1973 case, investors lost their entire equity on default by the corporation on a million dollar mortgage; in addition, the withholding taxes owed to the Treasury Department had not been paid. One alleged reason for the disaster was failure by participating doctors to obtain local hospital privileges. Additionally, the promoters overestimated the number of prospective patients who would seek medical services ten times over.

It is therefore not surprising that the condominium concept looked attractive to doctors interested in purchasing interests in new professional medical buildings, especially those in which they wished to practice. With the condominium form, the cooperative aspect of the venture is more clearly defined and protected by statute, because each investor gets a deed to his own unit entitling him, by statute usually, to mortgage it separately and to be assessed and taxed separately by the local property taxing authority. Thus the worries about the default in payment of a single building mortgage are eliminated because of separate condominium unit mortgages. If another doctor fails to pay his property taxes on his own unit, the other owners are immune from foreclosure on their own units. And, as we shall see, other practical reasons abound for preferring the condominium format in group enterprises of this type.

USE OF THE CONDOMINIUM FOR MEDICAL BUILDINGS

Developers of the condominium format seek to attract not only those doctors who are newly ready to enter practice, but also those now practicing out of their own homes or in rental quarters in nonprofessional buildings, or practicing in rental quarters in professional buildings. Additionally, doctors (and other investors) who now own professional buildings through partnership, corporate vehicles, or singly, whether they practice on the premises or not, may wish to consider conversion of the structures to condominium ownership.

It is a notorious fact that doctors are probably among the most difficult group of tenants for a landlord to satisfy. Rarely will you talk to a doctor whose office is run on a rental basis that you don't listen to a tale of immense dissatisfaction. Among the more specific complaints are allegations of unreasonable increases in rent at the end of leases; problems in getting approval for major electrical and plumbing work that would permit new or better equipment; need for better space partitioning; and inadequate landlord servicing, especially in buildings that are primarily residential. Whereas 20 years ago it was rare for a doctor to move his office (usually because of his heavy dependence on a confined neighborhood clientele), today that is no longer true, especially among younger doctors. This mobility factor, added to general dissatisfaction with renting, creates an immense market for planned, professional, condominium medical complexes.

In this connection, communities experiencing a shortage of doctors should consider giving liberal government loan inducements to encourage doctors to purchase new condominium office units and thereby own a stake in the community, rather than entering on a mere rental basis that would be simple to terminate. State and federal condominium purchase programs should be originated that would give 100 percent financing on liberal interest terms to doctors moving into areas without practitioners. Existence of attractive, fully equipped, new professional buildings able to service a wide area of residents otherwise without adequate medical care may well be aided considerably by the condominium concept. The author has been informed by letter from the U.S. Department of

Housing and Urban Development that the condominium form of ownership is not permitted under the Title XI Program for financing group medical practice.

Developers should also be aware that doctors generally like to be associated with members of their own profession engaging in many different specialties. Opportunities for discussion and comments, the flow of patients from recommendations of other doctors, the general benefits of social cordiality among professionals, all are attractive considerations that foster group arrangements. Probably the most important other reasons for medical practitioners to consider the condominium are the benefits of convenience, independence, and location. Let us look a bit more at each of these factors.

MEDICAL AND DENTAL CONDOMINIUMS: CONVENIENCE

Probably the chief observable difference between medical buildings and ordinary office structures is the degree of intensification of layout. Partitions, partitions, partitions are what we note immediately in the precious confines of most doctor suites.

Intensive partition spacing usually is required in the medical professions for each practitioner to service several patients at one time, usually between two and four. The doctor must therefore have as many separated examining rooms as necessary, in addition to several washrooms for patients and his own convenience, perhaps his own laboratory, and facilities for special examinations and treatments that may have to be setoff by walls. Examination of medical buildings shows radically different partitioning for specialties; space for radiologists varies completely from an internist's requirements. Inadequacy in partitioning can be of several sorts:

1. Improper division of space that does not provide adequate room for patient or doctor movement, entrance or exiting.
2. Inadequate ventilation, sound-proofing, and warming and cooling. How many times have we visited professional buildings in the summer months and found insufficient air conditioning in partitioned areas?
3. Inadequate electric and gas power and outlets, including technical requirements for special needs, such as compressed air. Doctors dislike rental terms requiring landlord permission for installation of new equipment or replacement of old, because of the continued likelihood of major rent increases under such circumstances.

Medical buildings examined by the author seem to be built with one of two notions by developers who rent premises to doctors, even if the particular needs of specific tenants are known before renting. In a few cases, especially older buildings, the builder must have thought that the needs of the medical profession were going to remain static for the next fifty years; there is just that little flexibility left from the kind of construction materials used in arranging space divisions and room sizes. The more modern noncondominium builder often goes to the other extreme. He either does not provide adequate space allocations, or he builds flimsy dividing partitions that suffer from one or all of the inadequacies of partitioning we have discussed above. He seems to be worried as much about later tenants as his current ones.

The condominium developer approach seems to be quite different in a large number of instances of newly constructed medical professional buildings. To attract purchasers developers usually spend considerable sums obtaining optimum architectural layouts to suit purchasers. More versatility is generally permitted purchasers for a rather obvious reason. *The builder does not have to worry about different space requirements of subsequent tenants,* because he is finished with the venture once it is sold to the doctors.

Doctors dream of the perfect locations someday, just as every professional in the scientific field does who must deal with the public. Selling a doctor a condominium office unit presupposes attention to this factor, to create conveniences that are not available elsewhere and that are tailored to the needs of his profession. The placement of good clinical laboratories and pharmacies in the same building sometimes can be helpful, because of difficulties of some localities in attracting strategically located enterprises of these types that must service the medical profession and its patients. In one nine-story medical condominium in western Florida, the ground floor contained a clinical laboratory, a physical therapy laboratory, and a pharmacy. Interestingly, the company managing the building owned as a unit the entire floor involved, which it leased to a single service company. The sharing of such buildings with unit owners engaging in other scientific professional occupations such as dentist, and optician, provides a built-in, noncost advertising factor because patients of each will note the existence and specialty of the doctors on premises.

Many conveniences are possible by condominium sharing of common areas. For example, a children's supervised playroom may be provided to service all unit owner patients. The cost of such facility, including employee salaries, could be made a common expense. The use of such a facility can remove some of the overcrowding of individual unit waiting rooms resulting from groups of children accompanying parents. Commonly owned space could house expensive technical equipment that can be conveniently shared by all or several unit owners, under condominium arrangements we have already discussed in our coverage of condominium regime management techniques. Doctors need not engage in group practice to derive these benefits, if the flexible condominium format is employed.

The condominium form only permits such conveniences. Doctors must examine each offering presented to be assured that real quality at reasonable cost is actually being offered to them, and that the developer is not providing the same old problems under a new name.

MEDICAL AND DENTAL CONDOMINIUMS: INDEPENDENCE

Many doctors, irrespective of location, have found it necessary to practice in two- or three-man partnerships. One underlying reason is recognition by medical and dental professionals that they also need vacations, a few restful weekends each month, a full night of sleep on a regular basis, and substitutes when illness strikes them. Yet, the partnership mechanism means loss of independence on many levels such as decisions on selection and purchase of equipment, rental of space, regular days off, vacation periods, insurance on the partner's life, and many other matters.

The condominium does not present a panacea for all these problems. Nevertheless, a careful set of bylaws can provide for such matters as emergency substitute services among doctors, cooperative services during vacation periods and other problems that can plague a doctor when he practices alone and wishes to take a vacation or must be absent for other reasons. With the condominium concept, these problems can be solved without the doctor's having to sacrifice his independence on vital matters for the entire year by way of a partnership with others. In addition, practitioners generally are most sensitive about the confidentiality of income information; the latter information can be safeguarded with independent condominium ownership, but certainly not when engaging in a partnership practice. When the doctor is away from his unit, condominium management can provide janitorial and security services and telephone and mail conveniences.

The author has known of medical and dental practitioners in partnership who in later years became quite argumentive when one wished to go into semiretirement and work only two or three days a week. By partnership agreement they each shared specific percentages of total income, creating an immediate problem among the participants. Often it is in the later years of practice that such problems arise, from age, illness, or just plain differences in temperament. The independent condominium unit practitioner could, in similar circumstances, rent his unit for one or more days per week, receiving income thereby, subject to the requirements in condominium bylaws. But the latter should not be an obstacle of proportion if the original regime documentation has been expertly drawn with a view toward future eventualities.

Let us assume, as has happened, that a young member of a general practice dental partnership wishes to study orthodontia work on his days off, hoping to switch to such specialty. A hide-bound partnership agreement may require the consent of his partners. The dentist who independently owns his condominium unit would ordinarily not be faced with such a formidable obstacle that might endanger his career for many years.

MEDICAL AND DENTAL CONDOMINIUMS: LOCATION

The following factors would seem fundamental in evaluating the present or contemplated location of a condominium medical building:

1. Accessibility.
2. Nearness to hospitals.
3. Proximity to other services.
4. Distance from medical and dental schools.
5. Parking facilities available.

In many areas of the country, medical professional buildings are best placed away from the heaviest business center of a community, but on a well-located key traffic route. Thus land costs may be reduced without suffering from inconvenience in reaching the area. The building should be constantly visible to the public when shopping, commuting, or just passing by. The potential patient coverage estimates should be made by experts, not imaginative builders.

Hospitals should be easily reached from the condominium building. Many doctors must have access to hospitals for their patients, as well as advanced equipment not otherwise available. Millions of Americans carry some form of hospital cost insurance that insures for procedures that would not be covered if conducted at a professional building center not qualifying as a hospital. Moreover, patients would soon shy away from doctors, especially specialists, if they were not attached to nearby hospitals. Although patients could be taken on long trips to other hospitals, many would not wish to be out of easy visiting range of their families and friends. One of the first professional office condominiums in New Jersey was a twelve-suite building directly across the street from a hospital.

Depending on the type of community involved, doctors may require buildings close to certain supporting specialties. In a cosmopolitan large city one can assume the existence of many pharmacies, clinical laboratories, and dental mechanics. In smaller areas, long trips may be necessary to reach the services that supply doctors as well as patients with needed materials. Close proximity to such nonmedical professions must be considered as adding additional value to the particular location.

Many doctors, notably more advanced practitioners, find it stimulating or even essential to be connected with training programs in medical or dental schools, either by serving on the faculty or by keeping afresh of new developments by attending regular or special lectures. If a professional medical building can be located within a reasonable distance to major schools, this is certainly an additional factor of substantial worth that enhances the financial value of the condominium and could attract specialists of greater prestige.

A location should be chosen where adequate parking can be provided. There are usually four kinds of parking to be considered when reviewing adequacy in a medical professional building. The same considerations may well exist for many other kinds of office facilities serving the public.

1. Adequate parking for patients means enough locations set apart. Too many professional buildings cater mainly to doctor and staff cars with grossly insufficient space left for patients. Patient parking should be immediately adjacent to the facility, with ramps for wheelchair cases. Preferably the parking area should be on the entrance level, easily entered and marked accordingly so that this information is visible to street traffic.

2. Full-time and part-time supporting staff, nurses, secretaries, clerks, technicians, and so on, should have their own parking area. This probably need not be conveniently located at entrance level or immediately adjacent to the condominium building.

3. Doctors should have space reserved close to the building, at a convenient level, preferably near an entrance permitting prompt arrival and departure. Practitioners may prefer entrances different from that used by the general public, and the location of their parking spaces should be reviewed in that connection.

4. Delivery and other commercial trucking vehicles should be provided with adequate space if possible. Typically they are not, and are

left to park any which way that suits the moment, often blocking traffic in the parking lot or taking spaces reserved for professional staff.

The adequacy of parking overall depends on the number of staff members and the number of patients they service, and planning that really comprehends the aforementioned group of needs.

In some localities it is important also that the building be located close to public transportation.

MEDICAL AND DENTAL CONDOMINIUMS: MIXED BAGS

Not only can developers offer units for outright condominium unit sale, but also they can offer straight rentals, or rental terms containing options to purchase. Sometimes this is done as a speculation by the builders in future rentals or sales. Sometimes such procedures evidence difficulty in selling.

Prospective purchasers should have their attorneys thoroughly evaluate the condominium documents to determine what will remain of lingering builder controls on operation and management, and whether the right of first refusal or approval is to be applied in a reasonable way as to future purchasers or renters selected by the builder or his assignees. Many of the benefits of condominium ownership might be lost if a large number of occupants are solely in a direct lease arrangement with the developer, even if options to purchase are contained in their leases. If a builder sells units to nonscience occupants, prospective doctor purchasers should be aware that condominium government decisions will in the future have to cope with the business requirements of such occupants as well.

EVALUATING CONDOMINIUM UNITS FOR DENTISTS

Condominium developers should be acquainted with some interesting attitudes and preferences affecting the dentistry profession that may not be obvious to the layman. Dentists are much less apt than M.D.'s to accept space in buildings housing other general practitioners, especially in smaller communities. The dental profession still seems to depend more on close neighborhood clientele than medical practitioners. (One possible reason could be that children often visit the dentist alone for continued treatment and must be within easy walking distance.) A concentration of general practitioners might stir the fear of immediate competition, which is not to the liking of many dentists.

Dentists participating in new professional building complexes tend to be younger on the average than their medical counterparts. It is not often that an older dentist relocates a considerable distance from his previous location, probably demonstrating concern for possible difficulties and handicaps in starting a new practice or one that might begin with only a small nucleous of former patients.

It is generally easier to sell an entire dental practice with a high percentage of patients choosing to remain as patients with the incoming practitioner than would be the case if an M.D. sought to do the same. For this reason established dentists often take advantage of constancy of patient buildup by fully subleasing rented premises to other dental professionals; in the case of condominium, the opportunity to sell their unit at a higher price is increased by the extent their practice has thrived. Dentists owning their own offices who build practices to the maximum sometimes have subdivided their space and entered partnership or special agreements giving themselves preferential dentistry income and managerial authority as well as full rental income as the property owner.

In the condominium containing dental units, one may expect later requests to the board to subdivide units or to lease portions thereof to other dentists. Bylaws should contemplate such problems, either by a clear prohibition, if this would be the majority outlook, or by provisions specially tailored to permit dentists to maximize profits by sharing space in a wide variety of ways. Dentists should be wary of purchasing a condominium unit in which later profit opportunities will be curtailed by rigorous bylaws.

Dental surgeons and other specialists do sometimes concentrate in particular buildings or neighborhoods in which the surrounding population and general dental practitioners can support their activities. It would seem best to attempt to obtain dental specialists as well as general practitioners in the same condominium, to provide a full-service building, although this depends on the area and population being served.

RESEARCH CENTER CONDOMINIUMS

There have already been a few instances in which condominiums have been organized primarily for occupants engaged in professional scientific research. For example, a group of universities in one case pooled together to form a scientific research center in which at least one structure was a condominium office building. If can be expected that different categories of university and business research will, in the near future, be widely organized and administered on a condominium basis.

There are several reasons why the condominium concept may become important in this area of development. Most of these reasons relate to the central and overriding pressures of massive expenditure impositions if any person, college, or business firm wishes singly to attempt to build an adequately equipped scientific research center to meet their own requirements.

Computer technology has become an absolute essential for any modern scientific research program. Access to sharing of computer equipment is almost taken for granted when developing such buildings. In the years to come the miniaturization of technical equipment will enable scientific and research business personnel to make immediate, complex testing operations on site, if adequately connected to a larger centralized facility based on computer technology. Even medical practitioners may be expected regularly to conduct comprehensive examinations of patients by quick hookups of miniature electronic and chemical equipment that will be tied into a central mechanical artery system that will immediately respond to the data fed by doctor and patient.

Many scientific buildings will require connecting corridors leading to essential facilities that are necessary during operating procedures, with such corridors being common areas utilized by many participants, just as computer areas and connecting terminals and wiring will be commonly used.

Scientific buildings will present additional challenges. Differing specialists will require facilities taking up quite varying volumes of space. Ordinarily accepted space standards for offices cannot be taken for granted as satisfactory for research specialties that have to use equipment of unusual sizes. One of the problems flowing from this fact is the potential effect on resale value and leasing if the condominium unit purchaser wishes to sell or lease an unusually sized unit that has been uniquely structured to his special requisites.

Another distinguishing feature of research buildings is the need for protective covering, vents, and insulating materials so that dangerous or odoriferous research products or by-products do not contaminate areas within or outside the building complex. This latter factor can be an expensive burden at the time of construction and heighten maintenance costs. The condominium developer must determine how much of such material often built into walls should be made part of the unit itself and thus be the responsibility of the unit owner rather than the common regime. There will be situations in which it will be advisable to establish that certain insulated materials and protective vents are a common responsibility of all unit owners to be maintained by the board of managers as common expenses.

In constructing scientific buildings it has already been shown by experience that prospective occupants are interested in such prospects as:

1. Access to scientific libraries within the building complex or close by (with libraries jointly owned and maintained by common expense probably a future development).

2. Access to other scientific facilities, including those at the university level near the condominium building.

3. Adequate janitorial services and sanitation programs keyed to the special needs of participants.

4. The nearness of universities that may offer part-time teaching and other positions to unit owners, as well as providing students for research center employment and training programs.

5. Centralized stenographic and typing services, which may not be needed on a regular, permanent basis but which may be required at special times for the issuance of reports and the maintenance of records.

6. Security for confidential research by sturdy physical division of units and an adequate security force on premises during regular working hours and after hours.

7. On-site warehouse facilities for storage of materials and equipment.

Most of the foregoing matters could be conveniently handled by a condominium regime developed for the purpose of catering to scientific research specialties. Past experience with such developments leads us to conclude that a substantial segment of the funding of the financial burden of construction and mortgage lending will be supported by universities and foundations, and by direct government assistance grants to create such centers. Investments of this type made on a condominium basis may enable a maximum use of premises, with little wasting of space, effective centralized management, and avoidance of duplication in scientific testing procedures, all of which are potentially possible by condominium ownership.

Tremendous opportunities loom for independent companies to reduce expenditures, and yet gain valuable opportunities to accomplish necessary research in a fully equipped environment. Most importantly, the independent structuring and operation of such research can be retained. With the efficient development of such procedures, many smaller- and middle-sized companies will be enabled to compete more effectively with more heavily funded, research-minded competitors.

INDUSTRIAL PARKS AND COMPLEXES

CHANGING PRECEDENTS

Anyone traveling through the United States can quickly sense the smelly and darkening pollution from industrial plants and groupings lying on marginal land rimming major cities, or deep within a city's orb because the once-upon-a time edge of a city has been surrounded by rings of new residential communities. Dependence on railroads and water transportation necessitated such concentrations of industry, until trucking and high-speed highways permitted decentralization to begin. Recently, outlying areas also have realized that inadequate protective planning has led to perilous ecological problems. The next decade may mark the decline in established formulas for construction, placement, and operation of industrial plants as we know them. Imposition of drastically expensive antipollution equipment will require greater cooperative efforts by industry in experimentation and implementation phases. For such purposes, as well as others denoted in this chapter, the condominium format may prove a new key tool of industry, as the revolution in techniques ensues as the aftermath of a determined and aroused public clamor for change.

By the condominium form, a group of independent manufacturers can establish central machinery for waste disposal, air and water processing, and other procedures to which most will be forced to turn. It would seem that mobility of tenancies and changing needs in ordinary rental of space would add exorbitant costs to provide this result. Full, noncondominium ownership would require each firm to provide these expensive facilities. The condominium procedure would permit institutional financing that is backed up by the security of first liens on the fee simple ownership of each manufacturer in his own plant and the undivided interest he owns in common areas, including the waste disposal system. Without a combined ecology program that condominiums can provide, small- and middle-sized industrial producers may vanish from the economic scene.

LOCATION

Public dissatisfaction with the appearance and results of industrial production has led to considerable difficulties for developers in amassing well-located land for new construction. As an additional problem, demand for concentrated business paperwork offices has created competition for space in the most attractive business centers. Building in close proximity to residential areas, even if permitted, will lead eventually to fight after fight against industrial production techniques. Anyone studying the development of industry and residential housing near metropolitan airports can be forewarned on this problem.

Beginning in the early 1950s, tax-starved suburban areas in large numbers stretched out welcome arms for proposed new industrial plants, often aiding financially in the development of land and services that would attract such industry. Heavy increases in population by young marrieds had suddenly cast the burden of new schools and services on such communities, pressuring for sources of revenue. The influx of industry to many bedroom communities brought in new groups of workers, many of whom became completely dependent on local industry. Cities sometimes competed by utilizing urban renewal grants for development of industrial parks for downtrodden, abandoned, vacant, or marginal land inventories within city confines.

Much of the industrial spread has been haphazard, often involving variances from local zoning controls and scandalous activities by those chosen as "sponsors." With the coming of wider public fear of pollution, the industrial developer usually faces immense hurdles whenever seeking new areas to develop.

Because of this difficulty in locating, industrial plants will more and more have to concentrate on special sites set aside for their activities. The industrial "park" and other complexes of industry may gradually become the setting for most industrial innovation and expansion during the rest of the twentieth century. Their location and appearance in the future is probably not typified by most complexes now in existence.

Concentration in limited locations will require maximum use of land and structures on a most intensive basis, with the highest degree of miniaturization possible. Cooperative efforts by industry within the complex will be essential to permit efficient operations and optimum use of facilities. In this pursuit, the business condominium arrangement may play an important role, by lessening the need of an individual company to obtain space, equipment, and services that are wasteful and duplicating when utilized on an entirely independent basis or under short- or long-term leasing arrangements.

A condominium could involve common use of parking areas, private roads, sidings, loading platforms, heating and air-conditioning equipment, computers, elevators, garbage disposal, and pollution-reduction plants, warehouses, or other facilities capable of common usage. Additionally, the very construction and allocation of space may radically differ from conventional designs that must provide for wasted space and duplication of efforts.

CONDOMINIUM CONVENIENCES

Merely comparing the same plant from the condominium viewpoint with rental or full ownership should not be done on a standstill basis. Besides the convenience and savings from use of certain areas on a common basis, the very nature of condominium ownership permits the potential for facilities that might never exist under the other forms of ownership.

Besides a common warehouse for record retention, a condominium regime might go one step further and provide a record-reading center and staff, with the result that records can be reduced in size and be made easily available in readable form at convenient times. Use of a central television system could send such information to each firm an instant after the request is transmitted.

We may in the future see airstrip landing fields located in the vicinity of condominium industrial regimes. The on-site or off-site strips could be owned and maintained as a common element by all of the participants.

Recreational areas for employees in all categories could be maintained on-site or elsewhere that would provide attractive working conditions. A substantial bowling alley that would be too expensive for one firm to underwrite might be an important convenience if financed through condominium common ownership.

RELATIONS AMONG OWNERS

In many complexes of industry there is a great deal of unfriendliness and dissension among industrial operators. Too often each vies with his landlord, or on his own, for maximum conveniences, with little regard for the conveniences or viewpoints of other firms. For example, many firms do not adequately maintain exterior portions of buildings, to the dissatisfaction of their neighbors. Parking, loading, noise, and odor problems continually cause friction. There is usually no regular effective forum for discussion of problems, although "park association" membership may supposedly be required in some cases to enforce terms, covenants, and restrictions originated by the developer, most of which are rigid, inflexible, and preordained in a manner inviting violation as conditions change. When the developer does not turn over enforcement of restrictions to an association, conditions become even more inflexible in many situations.

The condominium, with regular meetings of members and an elected board of managers devoted to real self-government with authority to face new conditions and problems, would appear to present the opportunity for more effective cooperation to solve important mutual problems when they arise. Statute-backed enforcement of bylaws on urgent matters protects all participants. If industry must rub against each other in concentrated industrial areas, the existence of condominium representative management may prove a soothing factor.

THE CONDOMINIUM AND SALE-LEASEBACKS

There has been, and probably will continue to be, considerable interest by institutional and other passive investors in obtaining industrial investments by way of sale-leaseback arrangements with operating companies Initial organization of an industrial park by way of condominium ownership can contribute several important factors to better protect the investors in such transactions, as well as aiding the industrial producer in continued, favorable operation on the premises.

As matters stand today, industrial parks and complexes often contain a wide spectrum of ownership relationships. Typically, the developer or his assignee may own outrightly a substantial percentage of the land and buildings that are rented under short- or long-term leasing arrangements. The other space is often owned outright by independent industrial firms that have purchased such property in fee simple, but that nevertheless are subject to underlying covenants and restrictions imposed by the initial developer that may run with the land. In some instances, custom develops, sometimes encouraged by a management company or by the initiative of the participants, whereby consultations among operating firms take place on a voluntary basis on such matters as the acceptability of new entrants who are to be rented or sold property by the developer, or who wish to purchase industry-owned land or buildings by outright sale from current operating users.

In many situations involving a sale-leaseback offering, the prospective investor relies most heavily on the credit standing of the seller who would become the new lessee. Many transactions have failed to reach consummation in the sale-leaseback field because of fearfulness by institutions to purchase industrial properties from smaller- or middle-sized producers with only average credit standing. The real property and improvements in such cases become prime backing as security for the obligations of the lessee. It would seem that an underlying reason could be concern for the continued value of the physical inventory of the land and buildings involved when judged against myriad complex relationships within the industrial complex that affect the appraised value of the property offered as a sale-leaseback. The investor typically stays away from the nontriple-A–credit-rated industrial producer. On the other hand, office building sale-leasebacks are much more conditioned on the underlying realty value, the latter importantly related to the wide varieties of replacement tenants available on defaults. Industrial buildings are usually too specialized and limited in usefulness to others in the event of lease forfeitures.

If a condominium exists from the beginning, or properties are converted to condominium, there could be a more palatable arrangement created that could actually increase the capability of individual properties being subject to sale-leaseback arrangements. An effective declaration and set of bylaws for government of commonly used areas and the solution of problems arising among participants could provide a stabilizing factor that would tend to remove some of the doubts ordinarily present when varieties of business ownership and realty use exist without a formidable basis for protective control of independence and for the solution of vexing problems that may arise.

The investor can be assured of competent management hired by the unit owners for *their* benefit, as distinguished from management hired by a developer that oversees areas reserved by the developer and commonly used by independent owners of plants. Once the investor determines that the business outlook for the debt is fairly secure on the near term, he must appraise the capability of the realty to house subsequent producers in the same or other businesses. One attractive feature might then be a well-run, well-maintained industrial complex in which independence is protected and each company avoids violating the rights of the others. The condominium setting can sometimes help to create such an atmosphere.

In the condominium, the right of first refusal in the board of managers is a much more formidable protection for incumbents than the mere voluntary expression of producer opinion, which is about the only control in some developer-dominated industrial parks. One important feature that should be explored by investors is the exclusive right of individual producers to have first choice in the purchase of other property in the complex that becomes available for sale.

The condominium form of ownership in industrial parks and complexes can actually contribute to greater value of individually owned properties because of their increased capability for the sale-leaseback arrangement. However, from the very beginning of the drafting of condominium complexes, provisions should be made for potential sale-leaseback transactions if condominium unit owners wish to sell their properties in that way.

NEW TOWNS

One wonders whether some new towns that have been developed in the United States to date have placed their industrial segment, when they exist, much too close to residential neighborhoods included in the same overall development. In the future, it may be expected that industrial sites will be setoff more protectively from an ecological viewpoint, to carry out the mandates of pollution control while securing the benefits of employment for the local labor supply.

New towns are expected to be developed on sites in the United States that have had little residential and industrial construction to date, including vast areas of land tracts that have posed forbidding challenges to construction engineers, architects, public utilities, and others involved with land development on an economic basis. The more remote from established communities a new city is to be located, the more the industrial area participants must provide additional services ordinarily taken for granted in metropolitan areas. Industrial sites in our large cities are usually surrounded by amenities such as restaurants that are adequate for the immediate needs of the community. When executives wish to entertain incoming business guests, it is usually a simple matter to drive to better restaurants or hotels. A wide arc of service areas removes the need for intensive location on industrial sites.

However, in the new community in which distant industrial parks may be set in the future, there will be more need for immediate services of this sort. Restaurants, hotels, airports, local buslines, monorail systems, all may have to provide services to those who engage in production in the industrial areas on which the labor force of the new towns depend. Because of the dangers of community dependence on one or two key plants, it will probably prove more practicable to plan industrial sites that will provide plant housing and facilities for large numbers of unrelated industries. Under such conditions, the condominium method of ownership can prove valuable.

The additional services required in such developments, as well as other conveniences we have discussed, such as common recreational areas, can be furnished readily by the flexible form of ownership permitted by the condominium technique.

It cannot be said that any particular format will provide adequate facilities in the future for new town industrial development. Nevertheless, when our new towns are to be constructed in previously untouched parts of the United States, the condominium format must be given serious consideration as a technique for providing a satisfactory business atmosphere both for the owner and employees he wishes to attract to the new community.

The condominium method could also enable more than one new community to own segments of a large industrial center encircled by new towns that will supply all or most of the labor force. By this procedure the need for several industrial centers is obviated, with antipollution controls and other expensive requirements intensively committed on a cost-sharing basis. Within such an industrial condominium site, many varieties of ownership or leasing could be provided for production companies. Some may become unit owners, some may operate on long-term leases from government units.

CEMETERIES

CONDOMINIUM PLANS FOR CEMETERIES

With the tremendous growth in world population in the past hundred years, residential housing needs have been encroaching on once distantly located burial grounds that had been set aside when it became apparent that backyard and churchyard burial spaces could not provide for the deceased among the increased population. This was especially the case in urban and suburban centers where acceptance of smaller lots for single homes and construction of high-rise rental units foreclosed the rural methods for burial on one's own spacious land. Legislatures have formulated statutory requirements and safeguards for the promotion, construction, and maintenance of large public cemeteries, nurtured by religious and social customs rooted in many years of tradition. These rules mainly presuppose burial areas laid out on horizontal stretches of terrain.

This book is no place to discuss the propriety of religious rites covering human burial practices. However, much of current burial methodology is based on the practical knowledge that few ready alternatives are available or permitted. Funeral procedures today generally presuppose burials in a casket sunk in raw earth, internment in a private vault (usually in a cemetery), or cremation.

Heavily populated parts of the world have already been posed with the problem of widespread cemeteries that cover valuable soil sorely needed for tilling. Some cities in the Far East have permitted plowing on ancient burial places in the wake of new farming or housing needs of teeming populations. Archeologists continually find proof that ancient cemeteries have been desecrated and buried beneath expanding civilizations and the march to acquire valuable land sites. Alarming predictions of population growth expected throughout the world in the next hundred years have given rise in our own civilization to talk of moving cemeteries to distant sites to capture valuable land for needed urban growth.

Increases in world population may suddenly pressure for well-intentioned burial solutions that do not utilize present concepts of cemetery planning and development because of their agonizingly broad specifications for horizontal land use. Substitute proposals will hardly be accepted that do pillage to honor and respect for the dead, especially notions that are antagonistic to the idea that relatives and friends of the contemporary dead should be enabled to visit their resting places in an atmosphere of sanctity and serenity for reflection and prayers.

Condominium cemeteries may be a partial answer. Shocking?

The largest condominium cemetery development to date is the one planned for construction in Brazil, in which a huge high-rise cemetery may cost over 14 million dollars to build, and be 39 stories high. The building is proposed to be operated under a condominium plan. Quite interesting for its potential as a precursor of future thinking on the problem of burial sites, the building will have a reception area, more than a score of private chapels for services and wakes, flower shops, a rental plan for 30,000 ossuaries, burial vaults in large numbers taking up most of the floors, and even a helicopter pad for the convenience of visitors as well as families wishing to deliver bodies from distant locales of the far-reaching country.

The chief innovation allowed by the condominium form is the utilization of *vertical* space for burial purposes, whether the vaults are conveyed as condominium deeds to the family of the deceased, or whether investors as condominium owners of groups of units develop the space for special rental arrangements.

Many cemeteries in the United States sell land plots for future burials, with administration of ground care left to cemetery management, usually on a minimal basis that can be increased by the payment of a single or yearly extra maintenance fee. There would seem to be little practical need to convert such procedures to condominium conveyances of deeds if the traditional kinds of horizontal cemeteries are involved. However, if cemeteries could be constructed with neatly raised levels for burial mounds on carefully designed earth formations that meet personal and religious requisites, the condominium would permit issuance of deeds to plots placed above others. In such situations the main use of the condominium would be to divide space for ownership, not to interfere with established customs and techniques in management. Rather than move immediately to the radical design of the South American prototype, it is more likely that elimination of flat-land cemeteries will be the first step in making more intense use of burial areas. Perhaps statutory procedures will be enacted before long both to enable this form of development, as well as amending condominium laws to provide the legal means for implementing this concept.

As far as vertical condominium buildings are conceived as the answer to future cemetery needs, the purchase of a burial vault on an upper floor in a distinguished building that is well-located is not really far-fetched. However, health problems would have to be taken care of by new sanitary codes applicable to burial by utilizing airspace. Acceptance by major religious groups would be essential in most cases. Many persons at present may question the propriety of encasing bodies in upper space. Teeming population growth, however, could mandate such a condominium approach by the end of the twentieth century.

Many of the same problems would exist if it is ever found feasible to construct cemeteries in layers below ground. The condominium method would permit the deeding of exclusive cubicles of air space measured in a downward direction. It is dubious that such solution will find ready acceptance in Western civilization.

The condominium vertical cemetery would permit ownership without limiting plot acquisition to flat-land sites. Careful planning could provide an atmosphere of sanctity and respectfulness. Traditional condominium attributes in other kinds of ventures, such as management selection, would have to be formulated quite differently, probably with new statutory authorization.

PET CEMETERY STRUCTURES

The author is not aware at this time of any attempt to use the condominium format for the purpose of constructing vertical cemeteries for the burial of pets. Perhaps in the future we shall witness some efforts in this direction. It is also possible that this form of condominium can provide some interesting experience for later efforts in the human field. In the case of animal burial structures, endowments for perpetual care of the premises as a whole, in addition to the burial area, would seem essential.

Once again, the condominium method would be utilized principally to enable the purchase of airspace real estate, in this instance to house the remains of devoted animals.

LANDMARK OR RESTORATION AREAS

CONDOMINIUM TO SAFEGUARD HISTORIC SITES

In recent years much more attention has been focused on historic urban sites, often picturesque and contributing to a unique atmosphere for residents and visitors, that are threatened by the bulldozers of urban renewal or speculative builders. The condominium method of ownership may be able to contribute an interesting and effective way of helping to preserve such districts, especially where business firms wish to continue to engage in enterprises traditionally carried on in such atmosphere.

Let us assume that decay and inattention threaten the old-time harbor district of a coastal city famous for its quaint waterfront architecture, wharves, shops, markets, and fishing fleet. A combined effort by property owners, aided by government, could transform the area into a single condominium district in which the business establishments continue as landowners and proprietors, but within the strictures and confines of a condominium declaration and bylaws governing maintenance, restoration, and construction within the special restoration district. Tax abatement devices and funds from foundations and public donations could help contribute to the final result of preservation and enhancement of the unique area indefinitely.

There is also a distinct possibility that businessmen using the condominium form can help recreate a vanished type of community flavor on vacant or abandoned land. Taking the same waterfront locale, a group of restauranteurs and shopkeepers may together seek condominium financing of an entirely new international community with many varieties of stores and restaurants that would attract visitors to areas that had become commercially dormant. To maintain the required atmosphere, community cooperation is essential, and this would result from government of common areas such as roadways, green belts, gates, and shrubbery, and regulation of architectural preferences, outside color schemes, signs, and lighting, by a board of managers elected by the participating condominium owners.

The governing procedures permitted by condominiums can result in protection of the restored community. Merely to rely on "associations" of businessmen would be inadequate. Mere reliance on zoning and code enactments by government cannot possibly protect the day-to-day operations of each participant from the acts of others that comply only technically with government edicts. Single condominium management for the entire complex can more effectively assure protections in line with the purposes of the declaration and bylaws.

The condominium restoration development can emanate from other motivations. Businesses, such as restaurants, theatres, and hotels, might own properties in the surrounding areas that have been on the downgrade. Each may wish to build an outlet in the restored area, even if only to advertise their products or services to stabilize or increase the value of their more extensive property nearby. In case of complete removal later to the restored area, a portion of the new investment might be eventually recouped by the increased price obtainable on the resale of the other realty owned nearby.

The flexibility of condominium ownership is once again apparent when considering landmark and restoration projects. By no means should it be assumed that this method alone should be employed in planning these developments. However, the condominium format can achieve certain benefits, as described and otherwise, perhaps not readily obtainable under traditional real estate ownership and leasing techniques.

PARKING GARAGE CONDOMINIUMS

VARIETIES OF POSSIBLE USE

There are several ways that the condominium form may prove helpful in achieving convenient parking needs when the parking garage itself is a total condominium, with space units within owned exclusively by participating unit owners, and the common elements comprising such items as traffic lanes, mechanical equipment, heating units, underlying land, gasoline tanks, offices, structural components, roofing, shrubbery, and other commonly used areas.

In almost all condominium parking developments, we can expect intensive vertical use of land, whereby ownership of exclusive space is not inhibited by horizontal land limitations that would have impeded spreading the planned parking spaces on a horizontal plane resting directly on the surface.

Mechanical means now exist for building subsurface and vertical parking garages using a variety of new engineering and architectural methods. Most utilization of space has been by a single overall owner renting parking spots on a daily, monthly, or yearly rate to regular customers or transients. Whereas maintenance of ground-level parking areas is relatively cheap, the cost of maintenance and repair of automated facilities such as car elevators and lifts is quite high, to say nothing of the large expenditure for construction of vertical garages in the first place. Land costs make many small garage undertakings in the central city or other crowded locations prohibitive, leaving little alternative for most business firms but to pay high rental costs for business parking facilities not available on company premises.

Each business firm contemplating purchasing condominium parking spaces should first conduct a financial cost analysis that takes into consideration general efficiency as well as immediate dollar differences. For example, a company having troubles attracting employees to its site because of developing transportation and parking problems must weigh the gains from planned parking facilities against this factor, again often not easily computable in dollars and cents.

The following are some parking needs that may be solved by the purchase of condominium parking units for business use:

1. Several department stores, planned or in existence, are in need of parking space for customers and employees. Land availability and cost leave little alternative but to use vertical space. Roof space and underground facilities of individual stores cannot conveniently be used. Reservation of several floors of a vertical garage may help solve the problem, the condominium format assuring continued ownership without landlord's rental increases, good customer servicing by condominium employees, and maximum store space utilization for selling merchandising.

2. Local businessmen might wish to purchase condominium units and not rent space as the alternative. Quite often, ground parking areas are temporary sites pending sale as construction sites. The condominium would assure continuance of parking.

3. Investors might syndicate construction of a parking garage, taking ownership of groups of units intended to be rented by them to local businesses. The condominium format eliminates the need for personal management of the owned parking areas, because the regime will hire and maintain an adequate labor force to service all units. The bylaws in such cases should provide the order of priority given customers in locating their cars, in order not to give unreasonable preferences on incoming business to any particular investor unit owners over others.

A major tax problem for horizontal parking garage investors has been the unavailability of depreciation deductions that amortize the cost of land. Although this problem remains with all realty acquisitions, the construction of vertical parking facilities will permit write-offs of the cost of improvements, as in the case of any building and its components. The shared cost of the land purchase may reduce the nonamortization factor considerably. If substantial bank financing is obtainable for condo-minium unit purchasers, a tax shelter can be secured that could make the investment quite attractive.

If the unit owners have invested in large areas of the garage, their attention to voting and management is probably assured. However, if most owners of a large parking development each own only a single unit, a problem may arise over attendance at meetings and concern for service on the board of managers. In the latter case, much greater empha-sis must be placed on the selection and authority of the managing agent.

The condominium vertical garage may also originate in a conversion by an existing single owner, with a spin-off of the garage by formation of a condominium dividing the total area into exclusive units and common areas. If the original owner takes back units, we have a condoback ar-rangement. The original owner might thereby be able to cash in on an immense buildup of appreciated value once his depreciation allowances decline.

SHOPPING CENTERS

EMERGENCE OF CONDOMINIUM CENTERS

Less than a dozen shopping centers have been developed as some form of condominium regime to date in the United States. They each contain small numbers of retail stores, and have hardly been noticed by observers as having special significance. But they are significant, indeed, for what they portend. It is quite possible that the condominium format will play an important role in ensuing years in the planning, development, financ-ing, and architectural structuring of small, medium, and immense shop-ping centers.

In few fields of real estate have we seen so much radical innovation as in the shopping center field since World War II. For one thing, devel-opers seem to be striving as much to create a comfortable and attractive atmosphere for shoppers as to give them well-placed stores. Going to many of the immense new centers built in recent years has begun to take on some of the fun of going to a fair, as much to browse and be entertained as to buy. Putting aside the economic justification for developments in this category, there is a definite social aspect inherent in these changes. That same underlying concept is seen in the popularity of the residential condominium which has brought recreational amenities and carefree living to unit owners without the personal need to cut grass, plow snow, and so on. The modern shopping center exemplifies the attractiveness to Americans of relaxation and recreation even when engaged in such chores as shopping. Going to market has become a family affair when a trip to the more modern shopping center is planned.

Just as condominium home living has become more than dwelling within the confines of a limited set of rooms apart from recreational activities, the contemporary malls, exhibits, and decor of shopping centers are an extension beyond mere shopping. In some ways we are returning to the excitement and discovery experiences of the medieval fair.

Before we discuss the economic changes that have led to the popularity of the newer shopping centers, it is well to consider that their very components and decor in the future will reflect, as already does the residential condominium, a radical departure from the past in American attitudes toward living and working habits. The condominium shopping center format is likely to aid in implementation of these changing attitudes.

A BACKVIEW

To understand the future potential for the condominium in the shopping center field, it may be best to retrace briefly some of the history of realty development of retail store centers. Changes have occurred which reflect economic and social patterns of the day, and which question the adequacy of the limited ownership and rental methods that were taken for granted for long periods of history.

Concentrations of population in central urban areas almost forced the location of shopping districts to be at prime points near the junction of surface transportation lines, near a railroad station, or some other place that was easily accessible. Single merchants or retail corporate entities, aided by institutional financing and the securities markets, shot their buildings skyward when more space was needed from increased population demands and the development in the United States of greater varieties of consumer goods.

Into rural and small town and city came chain store adjuncts of larger stores that had originated in the central locations of large cities for the most part. Because of the competitive knowhow and broadened lines of merchandise of these chains, their locations sometimes immediately began a new shopping area into which other merchants came as satellites. Typically they concentrated on both sides of what became a town or city main streeet. The idea of the main street two-sided shopping area, store facing store, was largely forgotten when newer centers, detached from crowded urban centers, were first built after World War II in more outlying areas.

Tremendous increases in suburban populations, and the universality of high-speed automobile travel on new, fast highways, encouraged retail store developers, especially the important chains, to open stores in projected suburban complexes. Some of the stores were large, planned to continue the atmosphere and layout of city landmarks. But in most cases distinctly new architectural and internal design formats were developed. Oftentimes, the larger stores were surrounded by a string of one-level retailers. The first centers had all or most stores facing a large parking lot, the latter being the most attractive new feature.

Around 1950, new mall centers occasionally began to appear that located stores facing each other, reminiscent of small town America's main streets. By this system, the land areas lying behind front stores could be rented at lucrative rates. Those stores situated on the front entrance needed two display openings, one for the back mall as well as the parking lot entrance. As this system was refined, the mall space became more valuable than space fronting on the parking lots. This tendency and trend accentuated with the expensive enclosure of mall areas with overhanging trussed coverings that permitted comfort shopping in a heated and cooled atmosphere made possible through modern air-conditioning and ventilation techniques.

With the value of such centers becoming more obvious, developers attempted to enlarge these centers horizontally on the farthest possible reaches. But this move cut into needed parking areas, and was not always successful because of the unwillingness of shoppers to walk long distances. If a major chain store was suddenly placed a long distance away, shoppers who went there might not also come back to the original shopping area. The horizontal limitations of shopping center development became apparent.

In the 1970s one of the newer solutions has been to build shopping centers with two or more levels of concentrated space usage, with malls on each level. The future of shopping centers would seem to be in more effective use of now largely wasted air space. We are in an era when vertical space solutions are being sought.

Almost all shopping center development at the present time is by construction by promoting firms that lease space to the incoming proprietors, usually under percentage rent arrangements, whether the stores are delivered as shells or completed. An exception exists when major chain stores do the development themselves, retain full ownership of their own stores, but lease the remaining store space as well as the mall areas. In the midst of these simple relationships have been inserted sale-leaseback deals of many varieties, as well as exotic financing devices such as those whereby a total construction loan is based on viewing the separate credit rating of individual store tenants. The mall areas are often constructed and maintained by intermediary firms who receive rentals from all store operators. The dimensions of cost for mall maintenance have become immense because of the security, decor, and wear and tear involved.

It is in this setting that we shall now consider the prospects for utilizing the condominium concept, rather than existing formulas.

WHY CONDOMINIUM

There are several reasons why the condominium method can prove helpful in the development of shopping centers.

1. The trend to use of vertical space makes it technically difficult to convey traditional fee simple ownership to prospective store purchasers. On the other hand, this can readily be accomplished by formation of a condominium.

2. The growing use of expensive malls and other areas used in common are now paid for largely by assessments and rentals levied on tenants or store owners. Included in such charges is a profit factor. This profit factor is enlarged when the developer or other owner of such commonly used space does rent the entire space, or portions thereof, to an intermediary firm that constructs and manages (or just manages) such areas. In the latter case the profit factor in assessments must include the original owner and the intermediary operator in their quest for overrides of income over actual expenses. With a condominium, such areas can be made common elements, with each owner possessing a fractional undivided interest in this space. This method may well reduce costs by eliminating the profit factors discussed above.

3. The condominium method would avoid the pressures and outrages accompanying percentage rental arrangements. If a unit owner's store pursues a highly profitable future, it need not share such increases with the shopping center landlord.

4. If the store owners operated under condominium ownership, a greater degree of control by store operators of management and operations is possible for overall center operations. Currently, the landlord and center tenants usually join a *merchants association*, often a requirement of tenants by lease agreement. The association may possess assessment powers under a formula often controlled by the landlord. In a

true condominium, self-government would be in the hands of the store unit owners without domination by any landlord or his representative.

5. Because of the leasing arrangement, major tenants are relegated to seeking leasehold mortgage financing for construction or purchase of premises. In many instances the terms of such loans are more costly and onerous than would be a first mortgage on the fee which condominium ownership would make possible.

6. Smaller stores with short-term leases are continually under the gun of lease termination, especially if the center is successful and has a waiting list of prospective tenants. Condominium owners have eliminated this problem.

7. The flipping of ownership of leased premises eliminates the availability of owners and management contemplated originally. Additionally, resales create pressure for new forms of profit by incoming owners. Often an understanding ear for temporary business setback problems just does not exist. In the condominium, the nature of the total enterprise and the participants would tend to remain more constant without the uncertainties of the policies of new investors or management.

PROBLEMS IN EXPANDING THE CENTER

With rare exception, developers of shopping centers leave vacant substantial portions of surrounding land for later development. In the ordinary situation, this may mean constructing more shopping center buildings once the initial undertaking proves successful.

Usually there is little voice in these new ventures from those tenants already ensconced in the center. The effects of intensification of land use and new stores depends on each particular tenant's location, merchandise sold, and ability to withstand new competitive forces seeking the attention of shoppers or offering the same wares. Tenant lease clauses granting tenants a veto power over new competition pose problems in restraint of trade that will no doubt in the future be clarified. When such contractual arrangements do exist, they may well be challenged by those claiming that they constitute unlawful restraints on trade. Thus, even by contractual attempts, the shopping center tenant probably possesses a minimal set of rights against new competition.

A shopping center formed as a condominium also might run into expansion problems. The developer may have limited the property subjected to the condominium master deed, leaving him wide discretion to build competing stores on adjoining land. For this reason, the condominium should be physically formed so that it encompasses so wide or

exclusive an area that it will remain relatively independent in its operations, and possess the distinct character intended from the start that is
aimed at attracting the public to shop.

In some instances the developers of condominium regimes may attempt
to gain power to expand the regime itself later to sell off their withheld
land, having obtained prior approval from inattentive unit owners when
the latter purchased their original interests. Some situations coming to
the attention of the author present grave legal problems, because of the
attempt to secure prior permission to later change the specific interest
in common elements that was originally conveyed and enumerated by
deed. It is questionable whether such practices are permissible under
the overwhelming number of condominium statutes in the United States
which apparently require a definite and relatively unassailable specification of mathematical ownership in the common areas. To do otherwise
creates a mischievous vagueness to fee simple ownership, certainly not
intended by most legislative draftsmen.

LOCATING CENTERS IN MULTIUSE BUILDINGS

Floors of shops surrounding plazas filled with water fountains and plants
and modern or period decor can be expected in the future to be located
in different portions of office or other complexes. Examples already exist,
and in some cases the buildings are condominium in ownership.

The condominium form can be used in at least three different ways
to accomplish such multiuse. In one situation the entire building can
be placed under a condominium regime, with one unit made up of all
office space, and the other of a shopping center. Within these divisions
could be traditional leasing arrangements, or ownership offered by
splintering the larger condominium units. The latter procedure should
be authorized in the declaration and bylaws, to avoid negotiating for the
consent of the other principal owner later. Whether the store operators
are tenants or individual unit owners, the space for shopping can be
separately owned and probably financed by real estate first mortgage
loans. Another way mid-building shopping centers can be formed is by
direct participation of all store owners as condominium unit owners who
share in the regime with owners of individual offices, and so on.
Yet another program would involve an office condominium in which the
shopping center in its midst is made a common element, with shops
rented for the purpose of securing a profit for the benefit of unit owners.
Throughout all these methods can be mixed passive investor ownership
and ownership by operating unit holders.

The ability to convey airspace, and thereby develop mid-air real estate by denoting fee simple ownership, can be accomplished by use of the condominium form.

We are definitely moving to an epoch that will see one kind of multiuse development outsize its predecessor, in the march to immensity in intensive land use. Both the increasing shortage of prime space and the increase in population, added to new breakthroughs in building construction, will heighten this trend in the years to come. The more extensive a development, the more its working or residing population will be in need of essential services such as shopping areas. Multiuse thereby becomes almost axiomatic.

MEETING TOPOGRAPHY PROBLEMS

There are already plans by developers to construct three- and four-level shopping centers that yield to the special topography of ground formations. Careful design can avoid physical exertions and the feeling of climbing, and allow customer coverage of a wider area and more store space than in ordinary centers. Spiral-shaped museums with nonstop elevators to the top have demonstrated that almost every visitor can be made to pass most exhibits in the easy walk downward.

In traditional shopping centers, the developer usually sold some stores and rented others, with entire parcels of real estate transferred on the major sales. Even if this was not the initial intent, sales of some or all of the realty loomed as an additional means for obtaining liquidation of investment when deemed necessary or opportune, as when depreciation allowances fade. Sometimes sales would be made of single stores to passive investors who continued a rental relationshp with existing tenants. At other times the developer was a store operator himself and transacted a sale-leaseback arrangement with an insurance company or other investor whereby a parcel of realty was sold and leased back, thus liquidating cash investment and appreciated value.

How will topographical developments, store over store in unusual formations, be able to produce the same wide choices for conversion of space to separate ownership that exists when stores all rest on flat land?

One way will be by use of the condominium device. With the creation of a total condominium, with each store a separate unit, a flexible form of ownership would come into being that permits the developer maximum freedom to rent or spin off ownership of parts of the shopping center in an efficient manner that need not prejudice occupants or owners of other space. By making the commonly used areas the condominium common elements, this method would protect the entire center in continued use of essential areas, irrespective of switches from leasing to ownership or initial divisions of owned and leased space based on marketing realities.

The condominium is a definite consideration whenever vertical development of space takes place. It seems unduly restrictive to build architectural wonderlands making economic use of topography, rather than flattening land, only for "all or nothing at all" real estate development; that is, either for full ownership of the entire development that could only permit parting company with property in total, or allow for continued total ownership for rental purposes only. The condominium adds a third dimension, the ability to divide fee simple ownership of vertical space.

MORE THAN SHOPPING CENTERS

Convenient to reach, convenient to park the car, drawing large groups of people, the shopping center has attracted to its environs more than chain stores and smaller shops. The regional centers sometimes include office buildings, professional medical centers, motels, and a variety of other nonshopping buildings. One Cleveland suburban shopping center has attached a cemetery. As for office building space, it is sometimes placed above store space in older centers. In newer ones, it more often stands out alone, often at some distant spot as a far end of the parking lot.

A great deal of confusion might ensue in some cases if a condominium regime included both an office building and shopping center stores, because of the differences in interest and approach by respective owners. We are talking about a single condominium that would be made up of separate unit owners for each office or office floor and each store in the shopping area.

A condominium might be made up of two separate units, the entire office building and the entire shopping area, with exclusive common areas limiting the mall and other special areas to the retailers. In this way, the roadways, parking areas, and other facilities could be shared and managed for the benefit of two owners.

If the shopping center and office building are each to be condominium by sale of units to participants, consideration should be given to having two separate condominium regimes that would be tied together through an easement agreement and unit owner association that would govern certain common areas on behalf of both independent condominium regimes. In this fashion, no majority of specialized owners could vote against the interest of the minority group in a prejudicial manner on most issues involved in internal operations. The use of restricted common areas, and exclusive rights applicable to them by each condominium regime, would assure some degree of independence in key areas that could not be disturbed by unit owners of the other regime.

We are going to see some interesting arrangements in the years to come, and the condominium technique may prove quite useful in harmonizing the interests of different participants.

ELIMINATING LARGE-STORE DOMINATION

In a great many shopping centers, favored treatment has been given larger stores in location; availability of center maintenance and security staff; wider latitude in quantity, quality, placement, and method of merchandising; location of lighting and signs; as well as in other matters. The condominium format can present a way for smaller retailers to band together to achieve harmony and efficiency on their own, without the need for the afterglow of larger stores. Although big-name stores are an immediate attraction for customers, there is usually little opportunity for smaller stores to innovate and develop in the shadow of the giant store. Groupings of middle-size retailers by condominium may provide a means for growth and development of new retail firms that could never happen in the present atmosphere of the typical shopping center.

Almost all important retail development in the United States, including the giants of merchandising, is now by expansion to new shopping center sites. New towns have and will further accentuate this trend. Without some new enervating force for young retail companies, they will be relegated to second-class citizenship in typical centers that you can almost predict by names of stores in particular locations.

Large-store domination is slated to grow to enormous power if the present trend in shopping centers continues. Middle-size and newer retailers looking for a means of competition with giant stores may be able to use the condominium form to combine their resources without sacrificing their independence. Otherwise, as each grows, the likelihood of absorption by the giants or defeat by overwhelming competition may loom as the only alternatives.

Shopping center developers and their member organizations would do well to probe the potential of the condominium in widening the opportunities for smaller firms in the ever toughening market place that has become the American shopping center complex.

OTHER CONDOMINIUM USES

EXAMPLES OF MORE UTILIZATION

Name a business venture and you can visualize possible use of the condominium method.

Airports may seem distinct entities. Now consider them in connection with condominium development. Two or more municipalities can together construct an airport midway between urban areas that are separately governed. Exclusive areas can be used by each city, with runways, control towers, and electronic systems made common areas. Or several airlines can themselves aid in developing an airport by purchasing separate condominium hangar units and subjecting themselves to condominium government of common areas used by participating airlines, government services, and special freight operators.

We have occasionally referred to warehouse condominiums. Here the possibilities are immense. Either for long-term storage facilities, for positioning current inventory, or for record keeping that is convenient.

Within a few years, after the immense possibilities of the condominium form are implemented in all walks of commercial enterprise, American businessmen will realize the tremendous aid that has been added to their enterprises by addition of this new real estate ownership device. Once the full mind and imagination of our business managers are applied to this flexible tool for development, its potential should achieve results that may alter substantially the attitudes and practices of business use of real estate.

INDEX